Smoking Collectibles
A Price Guide

By
Neil Wood

Layout and Design By
Amy Van Hoosier

Photography By
David Dilley

Published By

P.O. Box 69
Gas City, IN 46933

ISBN# 0-89538-070-6

ACKNOWLEDGMENTS

Thanks to the following people for helping make this book possible & contributing smoking paraphernalia:

Wes & Elaine Hart
Renee Martin
Wayne Stoops
Joyce Layton
Olde Tyme Toy Mall, Fairmount, IN
Jim Roush
David Dilley
Jim & Erin Richards
Mark Cole

Clubs you may be interested in joining:

On the Lighter Side, Inc. - International Lighter Collectors
Contact: On The LIGHTER Side
              International Lighter Collectors
              136 Circle Dr.
              Quitman, TX 75783-1824
Please send Self Addressed Envelope.

PLPG - Pocket Lighter Preservation Guild
Contact: PLPG
              11220 West Florissant, Suite 400
              Florissant, MO 63033

              Yearly Dues: $30

Table of Contents

Introduction

Welcome to the realm of Smoking Collectibles. Centuries have passed since the first clouds of smoldering tobacco wafted into a man's lungs-and today smoking is enjoyed throughout the world. An incredible assortment of smoking accessories and tobacco mixtures can be discovered across the globe, as so many cultures have adopted smoking into their daily life-style. Primitive tribes bellowing smoke through lengthy hand-carved pipes is quite a contrast to modern day implements such as electric-powered water pipes. Of course, many of us share the childhood memory of discovering a "grown-ups" cigarette-holding back tears as fits of coughing occur while we "puffed away" in some secluded hiding spot.

The time approaches when we again may need a hiding spot to enjoy smoking, as many "public interest" groups and organizations are rallying against smoker's rights. Long gone are the days when you could just "light up" anywhere. NO SMOKING has truly become a sign of the times, glaring at customers in stores, dining rooms, and public facilities everywhere. It is widely understood that there is a need to respect the choice of non smokers and limit the possibilities of fire hazards, yet the argument of when and where smoking may occur thrives throughout the media.

Will smoking eventually become "extinct" in the Western World? More than likely, the answer is no. Smokers are everywhere, and we all realize the fact that they become <u>quite</u> irate if they have no cigarettes. The hobby of collecting smoking accessories is becoming widely known-and attracts quite an amount of attention due to the "smoker's rights" dissension found throughout the country. Smoking is definitely a major facet of American culture. Consider this: Would James Dean have looked near as "cool" if he didn't have a cigarette butt perched precariously on his lip? We all remember General MacArthur's corn cob pipe held fiercely in his teeth. And just how did George Burns reach such a venerable age with a smoldering cigar stuck in his smile?

Items associated with smoking are already everywhere in the antique/collectible community. Antique tobacco advertising can be found at virtually any mall or show, and especially today there are countless collectible premiums offered by tobacco companies.

We appreciate your interest in this book, and as you explore the vast array of smoking paraphernalia throughout these pages, hopefully your knowledge and "burning" desire for smoking collectibles will be enhanced . . . Enjoy!

By Patrick Campbell

Smoke

Each of our vaunted advances had its prototype when the wilderness was king. The warrior had his buckskin pouch; perhaps the Royal Princess of his tribe fringed its edges much the same as her fair successor beads and braids the ones that hang there on the wall, beautiful yet useless.

Therefore, as from one pale brother of the fraternity of the weed to another, it behooves us to select our most ancient altar and our own private incense, for, look, ye, brothers, do two of us agree on what is best? And, breathing the comforting aroma, peruse these pages for what is good to us.

Like all other parts of the smoker's outfit have no beginning, the first tobacco presented to the explorers of the Western Continent being in the deerskin pouches worn suspended on thongs around the throats of the Indians. A curious feature of this happening is the fact that the Indian imagined his Great Spirit or God as "A man like the Sun," that is, pale in color, and brought to these white invaders his most precious possession - the pouch of tobacco.

DO YOU KNOW:

That nicotine was named for Nicot, Lord of Villemain, who made tobacco popular in France?

That nicotine is volatile and inflammable, and that nearly all there is in tobacco is consumed even before it goes into the smoke?

That nicotine is only harmful taken in its pure state and swallowed?

A Queer Smoke
Some of the Odd Substances Used Instead of Tobacco.

It is hard to think of anything else than tobacco in connection with pipes. Certainly hardly any substance with the exception of the "fragrant weed" is now in general use, in civilized countries, at least. But it is a fact well worth pasting in every smoker's hat that, taking the world altogether, from its dawning to the present time, tobacco, as it is known to-day, has been the least favored substance of all for filling the pipe-bowl.

Innumerable are the substances that have been adapted at various times by nations on the boundaries of civilization or in far-away parts of the globe for "pipe fillings." Here, however, is a particular list. The bark of the willow tree, the leaves of roses, wild thyme, lavender, tea, beet roots, maize, the roots of the walnut tree, rush, wood dust, hemp and opium.

And when it comes to pipes the variety of these consoling articles would make a list too long to be printed.

In China the pipestems are naturally of bamboo. In India leather takes the place of bamboo. Jasmine is used for pipestems in Persia, and in Asia Minor cherry wood is a favorite material.

Perhaps the most curious pipe-bowls in the world are to be found in the Philippine Islands, where, gold being the only metal handy, the inhabitants hollow out the nuggets and make use of them for their pipes. The pipes of old Rome, as antiquarians know, were made of bronze and iron, and the American Indians, it is needless to say, used stone.

A tribe in Africa smoke by digging a bowl-shaped hole in the ground, and bore others, corresponding to the stem of a pipe, leading to it. They lay flat when indulging in the fragrant weed. AND, REMEMBER WHAT THE SURGEON GENERAL HAS SAID." (ADDED 1994)

TAKEN FROM PUBLICATION PRINTED IN 1907

Suggestion for Smokers

An Opinion on Hygienic Smoking
By Edward Podolsky, M.D.

There is no doubt that smoking is one of the most widespread habits. To some people, because of a defect in their health, smoking becomes a problem, and a very acute one at times. When such a person goes to his doctor, he is simply advised to cut out smoking. Often that is easier said than done.

It is a comparatively simple matter, however, to introduce hygienic measures in smoking. The simplest and first is to use a cigarette or cigar holder. This prevents the constant absorption of nicotine and other derivatives through the mucous membrane of the lip. A holder also prevents the unhygienic habit of chewing the cigar end.

The matter of choosing a holder is an important one. It should be as long as possible in order to permit condensation of moisture in the greatest area possible. Drinkless attachments still further increase the condensation area. A still better improvement, it seems to me, is the filter cartridge which condenses and absorbs the tobacco moisture and assures a dry smoke.

Pipe smokers, upon medical advice, can exercise a great deal of intelligence in selecting a pipe. The shank of the pipe should be rather long. There are a great variety of drinkless attachments, and even the least expensive pipes now have them. Here, as with cigar and cigarette holders, a cartridge or absorbent material is preferable.

All good briar bowls are porous and absorb excess tars and nicotine. If a genuine briar is beyond reach, substitutes may be used. The cheapest is perhaps the corn cob. After it has absorbed all it can, it should be discarded. A fresh corn cob affords one of the driest smokes I know of. Cherry wood too has excellent absorbent quality.

Clays make desirable pipe bowls. Porcelain or clay bowls or bowl linings are very satisfactory. Meerschaum is the peer among bowl materials.

Cigar smoking is quite an art. Many smokers, with a wise expression and an all-knowing gleam smell the cigar and then put it to their ear, squeeze it and listen to its crackle. This does not mean a thing.

Proper curing is the key to cigar leaf mildness. Men who choose by light color may be on the wrong track for dark leaves may also be ripe and sweet and not necessarily strong. The best cigar is not always the one on the side of the box as is commonly believed.

The ashes should be gently flocked off the cigar, leaving some ash to bank the end against growing too hot. It is best not to relight a cigar when it has gone out. Try puffing awhile to try to get it going again. In lighting, use a wooden match and draw gently to start with. It is not necessary to char the cigar before you start smoking.

A cigar cutter must be used with care, if at all. Don't tear the leaf, but clip it clean. The more sharply pointed type of cigar should be cut.

Cigars should be stored at a temperature of about 65 degrees. Since cigars quickly acquire odors of surrounding substances, keep them only in suitable containers. It is best to store your cigars in humidors. This keeps out excess moisture and dryness.

These simple suggestions will bring safe and sanitary smoking enjoyment to every smoker.

Huffs and Puffs

FIRST PUFF-ORMANCE

I crept up the alley,
Climbed over the fence,
Moved very cautiously,
Felt very tense.
For in my jacket pocket
Was a new thrill for me:
It was a single cigarette,
My first smoke to be.
I reached a little corner,
Where I was out of sight,
Then took the weed from my pocket
And felt about for a light.
The match lit up in a flare,
That scared me half to death,
I held it to the cigarette,
And took a long deep breath.
The taste of the smoke,
Was pretty queer to me,
Cigarettes were not so good,
I soon began to see.
The smoke in my mouth,
Had a taste so stale,
That I drew it down my throat,
And it left me looking pale.
The smoke burned my lungs,
My eyes began to tear,
That I had been poisoned
I began to fear.
Things before me faded,
I thought I'd lost my sight,
Then-suddenly a low noise
Sounded on my right,
That must be dad,
Was readily my thought,
And a very painful lesson,
I soon would be taught.
The sound came closer
I was trapped like a rat,
Then out of the darkness,
Came a small grey cat.
My pulse beat slower,
Safe was my secret then,
Though I had not enjoyed it,
I knew I'd smoke again.

Jack Golditch. Our Office Boy.

Dear Editor:

After looking over the pictures of the girls smoking pipes in Smoke Signals, No. 5 I think that they might all take a lesson on how to handle a pipe from the snapshot of my daughter, Joan which I am sending along. If it isn't real he-man style, I don't know what you would call it!

*Walter E. Bishop, Sr.,
Rensselaer, N.Y.*

****

When I recently had the misfortune to crack the bowl of one of my pipes, I sawed off the damaged portion, reamed the smoke hole in the end of the shank to correct size and fond I had a rich-looking briar wood cigarette holder with a Vulcanite stem.

When I split the shank of another pipe, Improvised a brass ferrule by filing off a section of an empty cartridge case and fitting it snugly over the damaged end. It closed and covered the small crack and when polished to a bright luster, it added much to the appearance of the pipe.

When a Vulcanite stem snaps off, I file a new tenon on the end of it. I also make curved stems out of straight ones by slowly heating and bending them to the desired shape. They harden again as they cool and can be repolished.

In these days of shortages, no pipe part should be discarded. A good stem from a burned-out bowl may be fitted into a good bowl with a damaged stem, etc.

Pipe repairing is intensely interesting as a spare-time workshop hobby, and painstaking care may save many a smoke-seasoned favorite.

Frank Kenneth Young, Pewamo, Mich.

Meerschaum Pipes

Meerschaum, known in mineralogy as Sepolitei, is found in many countries, principally in Austria and Prussia, where it is used extensively in the **Manufacture of Pipe Bowls,** besides being a valuable export in bulk.

The name is of German origin and means "Foam of the Sea," as the ancients first found it floating on the waves and concluded from that fact that it must be sea foam turned to stone.

It is a chemical compound of silica, magnesia and water, and when dry the fine varieties will float, being extremely light in comparison to the bulk.

When taken from the ground it is soft and soapy, forming a lather by the application of water.

Each lump is wrapped in paper and dried very slowly. A yellowish brown bark which has formed itself is then removed, and all defects cut out; they are then rewrapped in paper and thoroughly dried, afterwards they are polished with emery paper, and brushed with fat to show their grain; the old story about genuine meerschaum when heated admitting of a fine needle to be passed through it, is like many other old stories-pure fiction.

The Spanish Meerschaum listed in the tubes is a recent discovery. The meerschaum being harder and darker, having veins of dark material-probably a formation of hematite or iron-imparting a peculiar beauty to be polished surface. This material will color as readily as the soft product while retaining the markings of the original mineral.

The Meerschaum Pipes are strictly first quality, free from all flaws and defects. Those with a screw joint have a bone brushing that is screwed and cemented in the meerschaum stem and receives the thread of the bone screw that is securely fastened in the Amber. This is a novel feature in this work, giving a large bore and better facilities for cleaning.

Those with "Push Bits" fit perfectly in every part, the stem being tapered to the bore of the meerschaum, making the connection absolutely rigid.

TAKEN FROM PUBLICATION PRINTED IN 1907

The Story of Meerschaum

A BLOCK OF RAW MEERSCHAUM

MEERSCHAUM is truly the aristocrat of pipedom. It is a natural mineral deposit that by a peculiar phenomenon has become imbedded under the earth's surface for thousands of years. The derivation of the word is from the German; "Meer"—meaning sea, and "schaum"—meaning foam. The only place in the world that Meerschaum of fine smoking quality has been found is in the plain of ESKISHEHR, Asia Minor. This was discovered about 900 years ago, long before tobacco smoking was in vogue. The estimated supply is now approximately half-exhausted.

The raw Meerschaum blocks must first be softened by a special process. Then they are fashioned by expert hand carvers, as only the finest craftsmen are capable of bringing out the fine appearance and smoking qualities of this precious material. They are finished by hand polishing with a special type of reed taken from the bullrushes. Then they are dipped in molten beeswax and hardened to get their high lustre and durability. (*This treatment must be administered with special care, as it greatly affects the beautiful coloring the pipe develops by smoking.*) Next, the Bakelite stems are cut by hand to fit each pipe and they are attached by special ivory threaded joints. Then they are enclosed in wooden cases, leather covered and plush lined, for protection.

There are many schools of thought regarding the smoking of Meerschaum pipes. Some advocate the use of false bowls, affixed to the top of the pipe, etc. We have found the best way of coloring the Meerschaum is to smoke it slowly and thoroughly down to the heel of the pipe, indoors, if possible, for a Meerschaum must not be subjected to sudden climatic changes nor re-smoked when it is hot. Any dirt, grease or perspiration on the fingers will show on the pipe. A chamois "jacket" may be sewed around the bowl for protection. A Meerschaum that has been well smoked turns a beautiful golden brown color which is the pride and joy of the real pipe smoker.

HOW TO TAKE CARE OF YOUR MEERSCHAUM PIPE:

The following simple rules will help you care for your Meerschaum: when removing the stem, hold the bowl in the left hand with the stem pointing toward the right. Now, turn the stem gently toward you—to the left. (See diagram.) When screwing the stem back on to the pipe, do not try to force it as they are made this way, so that, after a little use, they will be in perfect alignment. In case the stem is "over turned," do not try to force the stem around another time, as this will either break the screw or the Bakelite. Send it in to us for an adjustment which we will gladly make free of charge. A chamois "jacket" may be sewed around the bowl and shank for protection. A Meerschaum pipe that has been well smoked turns a beautiful golden brown color which is the pride and joy of the real pipe smoker.

Wally Frank

GENUINE PRIMA MEERSCHAUM

WITH BAKELITE STEM

This Genuine Block Meerschaum pipe is strictly a collector's item! Look at it under varying lights . . . see the almost indescribable underlying tint . . . a very faint rose hue. It is this rare quality that makes it a Meerschaum highly prized and sought after by connoisseurs. These pipes have the magnificent flavor that a veteran pipe-smoker enjoys.

Each pipe is packed in a full-grained, hand-tooled, Moroccan book-leather case, lined with chamois plush.

A pipe for the experienced Meerschaum smoker.

BENT

EACH PIPE IN INDIVIDUAL HINGED CASE

BILLIARD

APPLE

DUBLIN

BULLDOG

PLEASE SPECIFY SHAPE WHEN ORDERING

SMALL	STANDARD	MEDIUM	LARGE
Length Overall: 4⅞" Weight: ¾ oz.	Length Overall: 5¼" Weight: ⅞ oz.	Length Overall: 5½" Weight: 1⅛ oz.	Length Overall: 5⅞" Weight: 1¼ oz.

(APPROXIMATE DIMENSIONS)

ALL PRICES POSTPAID

1945 Catalog Page

Meerschaum Pipes

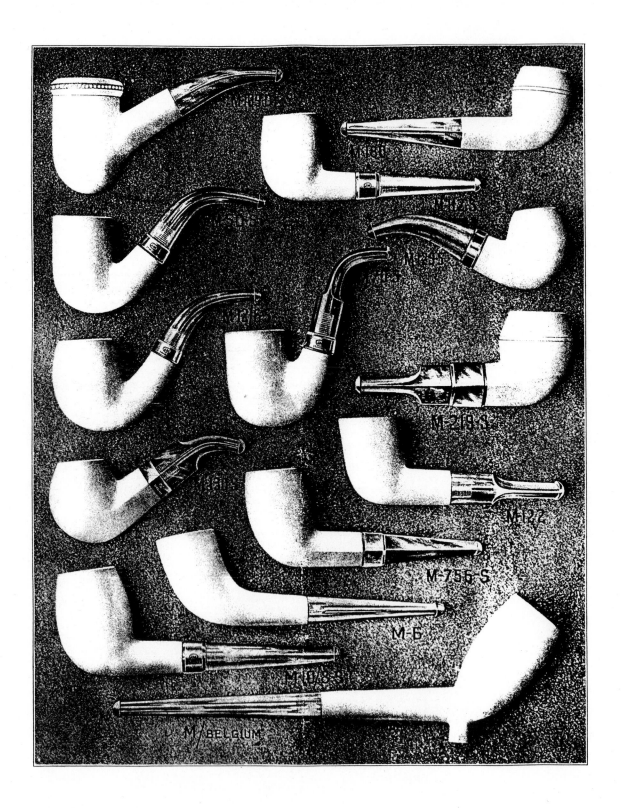

ALL ABOVE ARE ILLUSTRATED 1/2 SIZE
TAKEN FROM PUBLICATION PRINTED IN 1907

Meerschaum Pipes

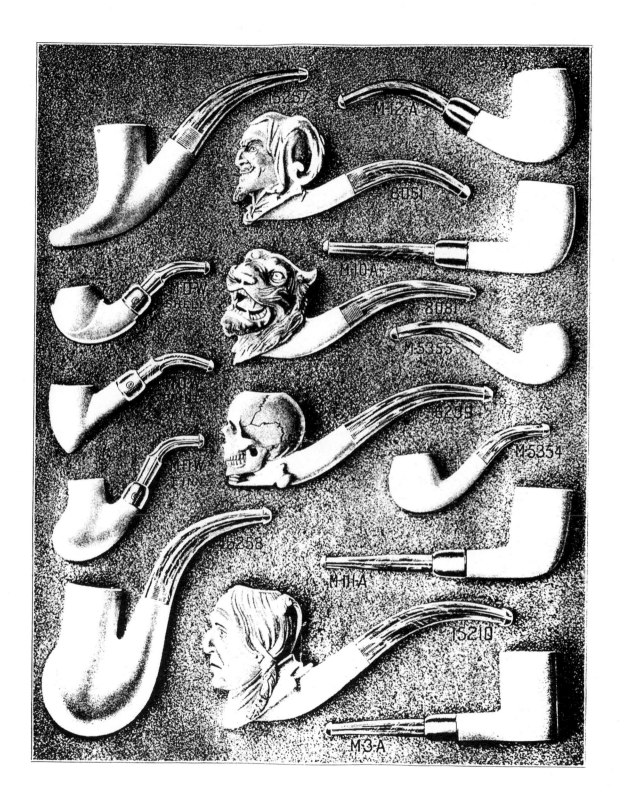

ALL ABOVE ARE ILLUSTRATED 1/2 SIZE

TAKEN FROM PUBLICATION PRINTED IN 1907

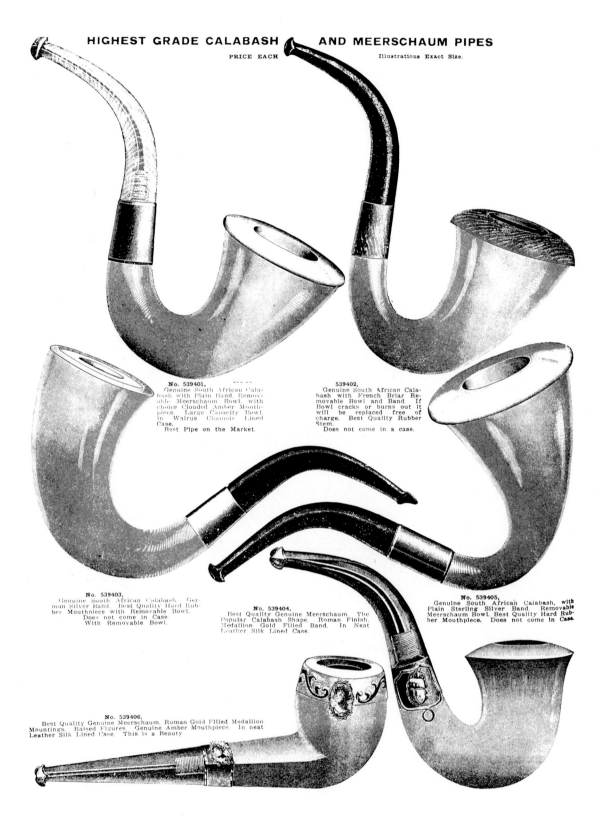

No. 539401,
Genuine South African Calabash with Plain Band. Removable Meerschaum Bowl, with choice Clouded Amber Mouthpiece. Large Capacity Bowl in Walrus Chamois Lined Case.
Best Pipe on the Market.

539402,
Genuine South African Calabash with French Briar Removable Bowl and Band. If Bowl cracks or burns out it will be replaced free of charge. Best Quality Rubber Stem.
Does not come in a case.

No. 539403,
Genuine South African Calabash. German Silver Band. Best Quality Hard Rubber Mouthpiece with Removable Bowl.
Does not come in Case.
With Removable Bowl.

No. 539404,
Best Quality Genuine Meerschaum. The Popular Calabash Shape. Roman Finish. Medallion Gold Filled Band. In Neat Leather Silk Lined Case.

No. 539405,
Genuine South African Calabash, with Plain Sterling Silver Band. Removable Meerschaum Bowl. Best Quality Hard Rubber Mouthpiece. Does not come in Case.

No. 539406,
Best Quality Genuine Meerschaum. Roman Gold Filled Medallion Mountings. Raised Figures. Genuine Amber Mouthpiece. In neat Leather Silk Lined Case. This is a Beauty

1915 Catalog Page

GENUINE MEERSCHAUM PIPES AND CIGAR HOLDERS WITH REAL AMBER MOUTHPIECE

Illustrations Exact Size.

ALL PIPES ARE PUT UP IN
LEATHER CASES
LINED WITH
SILK PLUSH

No. 539301, Plain Gold Filled Band.

No. 539302, Bent Calabash Shape, Plain Gold Filled Band.

No. 539303, Plain Gold Filled Band and Top Band

No. 539304, Fancy Chased Gold Filled Band.

No. 539305, Clouded Amber Cigar Holder, 2½ inches long, extra large opening.

No. 539306, Genuine Meerschaum Cigar Holder, 2½ inches long, with Plain Gold Filled Band.

No. 539307, without Mounting

No. 539308, Chased Gold Filled Band.

No. 539309, Fancy Chased Gold Filled Band and Top Band.

No. 539310, Fancy Gold Filled Band, Rose Finish Band.

No. 539311, Genuine Meerschaum Cigar Holder, 2½ inches long.

1915 Catalog Page

13

Vienna Meerschaum Smoker's Sets
Pipe and Cigar Holders
Excellent Premium Articles

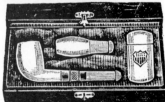

No. S1369, 3-Piece Pipe Set, viz.: 1 Vienna Meerschaum pipe, egg bowl, fancy nickel ferrule, amberine bit; 1 bulb shape cigar holder to match; 1 fancy gilt match box with spring cover. Assembled in an attractive rib cloth lined box, each piece in a nest. Makes a very attractive display. An ideal set for a premium plan or a similar proposition where big aparent value is wanted for a small price.

No. S1370 Pipe Set, 3 pieces, viz.: 1 bent bulldog briar pipe, gilt trimmed amberine bit, 1 gilt trimmed amberine cigar holder, 1 gilt fancy figured spring cover match safe, each piece nested in nicely ribbed cloth lined leatherette box with hinged cover.

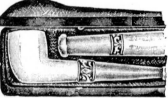

No. S1379. Smoker's Set, genuine Vienna meerschaum, consists of 1 4 in. pipe, Hungarian bowl, heavy round stem, rolled gold plated embossed ferrule, full size nice Amberine bit, and one 2½ in. cigar holder, round, full size, with good Amberine saddle bit and embossed ferrule to match; each set in plush lined chamois-lined case.

Genuine Block Meerschaum Student Pipe

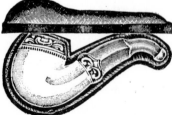

No. S134. Student's Genuine Block Meerschaum Pipe, heavy, bent style, gold plated trimming on bowl, ferrule to match, genuine saddle shape amber bit; 4½ in. Each in chamois leather plush lined case.

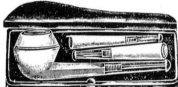

No. S1381. Pipe Set, Vienna Meerschaum, consists of Bulldog bowl, square stem pipe, flush amberine bit, one cigar holder and one cigarette holder to match, of a popular size. A combination destined to be the best seller in the line, handsomely finished, clean cut goods. In plush lined chamois-lined case. As well finished as high priced Meerschaum goods.

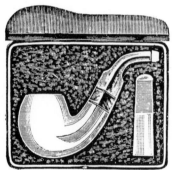

No. S1383. Pipe Set, genuine Vienna Meerschaum, egg shape bowl, square stem, nickel ferrule, bent saddle bit; a good, full size bent pipe; handsomely finished, fine quality, with 1 round cigar hoder to match. The two pieces are in a plush lined chamois-linen covered case; a very neat, attractive outfit.

No. S1380. Vienna Meerschaum Smoker's 4 Piece Set, one bent and one straight pipe, cigar and cigarette tapering holders, amberine bits with bright silver trimmings, egg and Hungarian shaped bowls, chamois-linen case, a very neat rich and attractive set.

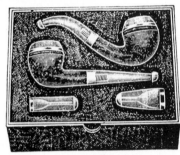

No. S1371. Smoker's Set, consisting of 4 pieces: one bent and one straight French briar pipe 4½ in. long, bulldog bowls, gilt trimmings, amberine flush bit; amberine cigarette and cigar holder to match neatly nested in velvet lined box. Very neat and attractive.

The Walter Raleigh Pipe Set

No. S9390. Walter Raleigh Pipe Set, consists of first quality briar pipe, bulldog bowl, mounted with fancy design, gilt trimming, ferrule to match, square stem, genuine amber saddle bit and genuine amber cigar holder with fancy gilt trimming to match pipe. In full chamois plush lined case. It is a handsome set, high grade in quality and finish. An admirable gift set.

Vienna Meerschaum Pipe

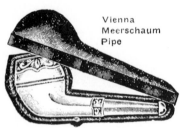

No. S1393. Pipe, genuine Vienna Meerschaum, very finely made and finished, grooved bulldog bowl, heavy square stem, flush amberine bit. This is an excellent shape and looks like the very fine genuine goods; heavy gold plated mounting on bowl, ferrule to match. Each in plush lined chamois-linen case; a pipe that will bring very good profit to the dealer.

1914 Catalog Page

Amber

Amber is supposed to be the petrified saps of certain extinct coniferous trees. It is not confined to any one country or locality, but is found in various quantities and grades in all parts of the world.

The chemical compositions are similar to that of camphor, and it is said to be analogous to the vegetable resins. It is classed, in mineralogy, with coal and other petrifactions. The color varies from that of honey to brown, occurring occasionally in shades of red, blue and green. Some varieties are almost transparent, while others are opaque and contain smoky or regular markings. At times the impression of a leaf or small insect will appear in large pieces. It occurs in round, irregular lumps, varying in size. It is hard and brittle, possessing negative electricity to a great degree. On being warmed or burnt it emits a pleasant fragrance.

The legendary origin of amber makes it the tears of the sisters of Phaeton, the luckless driver of the chariot or the Sun, who was destroyed by Jupiter for going too near the Earth. The sisters afterward become poplar trees.

The name is said to come from the Arabian "Amber," meaning like Ambergris. The Greeks called it Elekton on account of its electric qualities, while the Romans knew it as Succinum, from which they extracted Succinic Acid.

It was used extensively as an ornament and was supposed to contain magic properties; also as incense and later as pipe stems and mouthpieces.

Amber will melt at 536 degrees Fahrenheit. The greater part of amber supply comes from the Baltic, where it is thrown ashore after a storm; it is also found in the blue earth and superficial strata.

The largest piece of amber ever known weighed 27 pounds. The largest piece of amber existing at present is on exhibition at Imperial Museum of Minerals, at Berlin, German. Weight, 13 1/2 pounds. Value $75,000.

TAKEN FROM PUBLICATION PRINTED IN 1907

Amber

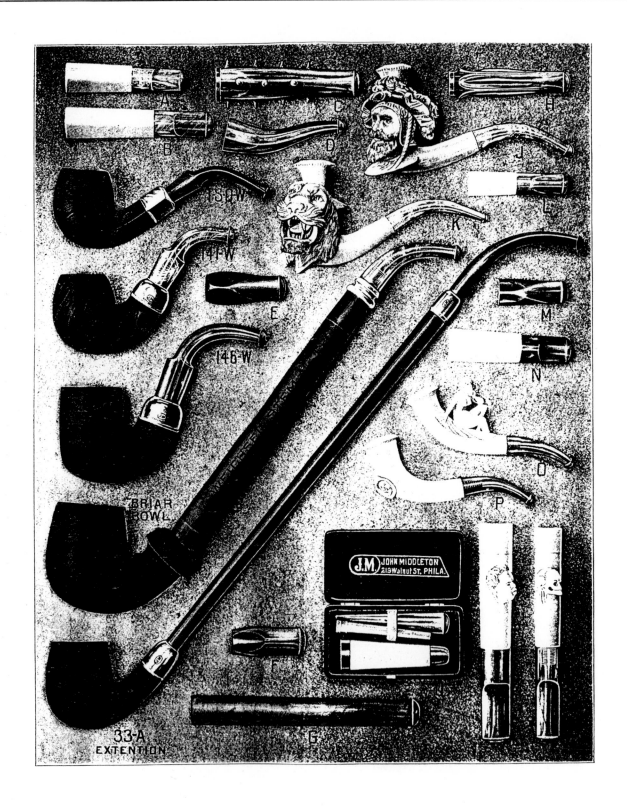

ALL ABOVE ARE ILLUSTRATED 1/2 SIZE
TAKEN FROM PUBLICATION PRINTED IN 1907

Miscellaneous

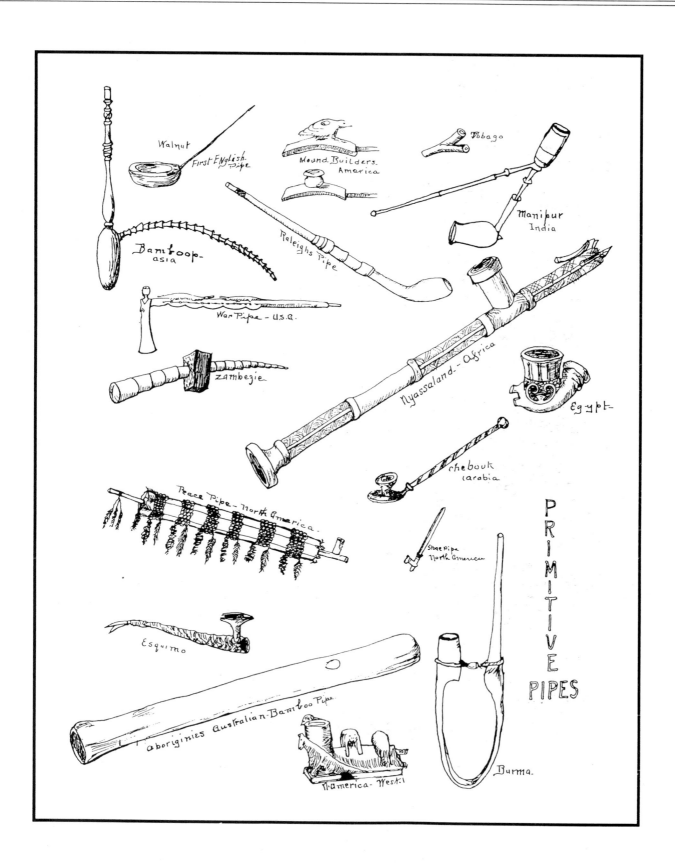

TAKEN FROM PUBLICATION PRINTED IN 1907

❦ ❦ CIGARETTES ❦ ❦

THE smoking of Cigarettes prior to 1880 was very much in vogue and created no comment or objection. About this time the method employed in advertising took a rather spectacular turn and the cigar industry, fearing the result, organized a movement tending to offset the popularity of its cheaper rival. The methods used were to the effect that all kinds of drugs, poisons, common or dirty materials were used.

This, however, is not true of the present article, perhaps more care and finer materials being used than in the manufacture of cigars. The trade movement was afterward continued and elaborated by the W. C. T. U. and various societies, aided at times by the medical profession, whereas, in fact, the greater number of doctors and students are inveterate cigarette smokers.

Of the many evils charged to them it is safe to say the majority are due to prejudice, and where harms result it is rather a reason for excessive indulgence than the true cause of it.

Many eminent physicians are cited as to the harmless qualities of Cigarettes in moderation, among them: Prof. Wiley, of the Department of Agriculture, Prof. Babcock, of Boston, Mass., Dr. Wm. B. Fletcher, of Indianapolis.—Extract from *Tobacco Leaf*.

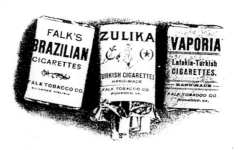

These Cigarettes are of tobaccos selected from the finest growths of the Samsoun District in Asiatic Turkey and the Caraella District of Turkey in Europe. The work is all done by hand and the result is a product that is almost perfect. These Cigarettes were awarded the Grand Prize at the St. Louis Exposition, and at the Lewis and Clarke Exposition, at Portland, Oregon.

Cork or Plain Mouthpiece

A. A. A.
Package of 10,   50's,

PRINCE
Package of 10,   50's,

SOCIETY BELLE
(Ladies' Cigarette)
Package of 10,   50's,

EXTRA FINE
Package of 10,   50's,

NATURAL
Package of 10,   50's,
Postage on 50, 7c

VAPORIA

A combination of Turkish, Latakia and Old Virginia Tobacco, giving a rich, fragrant, mild smoke. Rice paper.

20 in a package,

ZULIKA

A blend of Turkish and Virginia Tobacco, rice paper—a mild, sweet smoke.

BRAZILIAN

A long-cut selected leaf in a Tobacco pulp paper. A Cigarette having a distinct flavor of its own. Made from Tobacco of special importation.

20 in a package,
Prepaid in lots of 100

TAKEN FROM PUBLICATION PRINTED IN 1907

Nestor Cigarette Advertising Tin
13 ¹/²" x 19"

Satin Cigarette Advertising Tin
19"

Fatima Cigarette Advertising Tin
26" x 38"

Murad Cigarette Advertising Tin
28" x 39"

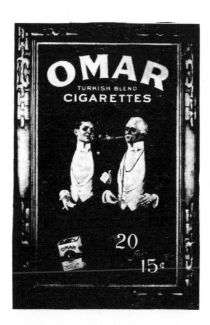

Omar Cigarette Advertising Tin
20" x 30"

Egyptienne Cigarette Advertising
Sign in Wood Frame
25" x 35"

Hassan Cigarette
Advertising Sign
22¹/²" x 28¹/²"

Zira Cigarette Advertising
Cardboard
16³/⁴" x 13³/⁴"

Sunshine Cigarette
Advertising Tin,
14" x 17³/⁴"

Ashtrays

Farberware Smokers' Articles

No. 2450—Nickel Silver Ash Receiver

Spun in Assorted Colored Glass
Diameter 3¾"

No. 2690—Ash Tray Set

Nickel Silver—With Jade Green
or Orange Colored Glass

Dia. Large Tray 4⅜"—Small Tray 2⅞"

No. 2453—Nickel Silver Nested Ash Tray Set

Diameter Trays 3¾"
Height Over All 4½"
Nickel Silver being a white metal,
these trays can be kept bright

Tobacco or Cigar Jars

Glass Jar, Cover Solid Brass
Brushed Finish
No. 1900—Height 4¼"—Dia. 3"
No. 1901—Height 6¼"—Dia. 4"

No. 2455—Nickel Silver Nested Ash Tray Set

Height 6"—Diameter 3¾"
Nickel Silver, being a white metal,
these trays can be kept bright

No. 2691—Ash Tray Set

Nickel Silver—With Jade Green
or Orange Colored Glass
Height Over All 5"—Dia. Large Tray 4⅜"
Small Tray 2⅞"

No. 2591—Hammered Polished Brass Cigarette Box

Embossed Ship Design
Copper Riveted—Cedar Wood Lining
Holds 100 Cigarettes
Size 4½"x3¼"x2" High

Silver Plated

No. 3450—Silver Plated Cigarette Box
Holds 50 Cigarettes

No. 3451—Silver Plated Cigarette Box
Holds 100 Cigarettes

No. 2592—Hammered Polished Brass Cigar Box

Embossed Ship Design—Copper Riveted
Lined with Cedar Wood—Holds 25 Cigars
Size 9" x 5½" x 2" High

◀ ◀◀ S. W. Farber, Inc., Brooklyn, N. Y. ▶▶ ▶

1931 Catalog

BL4081 Ash Tray Set........
A graceful figure of a goose finished in gun metal. Wings form a holder for pack of cigarettes. Removable ash receiver. Excellent value. Height 6 inches.

BL4082 Onyx Ash Tray.............
Genuine green onyx ash tray. Genuine bronze assorted figures of dogs, horses, birds, etc. Size 4 x 3½ inches. Special value.

BL4080 Genuine Bronze Ash Tray.............
Genuine dark green bronze parrot, two bronze asn receptacles. Green onyx felted base. An unusual, attractive gift. Height 7½ inches. Width 5¾ inches.

BL4083 Onyx Ash Tray..........
Genuine green onyx tray, deep weii. Modernistic. Genuine bronze figure of polo player, dark green finish. Diameter 3 inches. Special value.

BL4084 Bronze and Onyx Tray........
Genuine green onyx base mounted with dark green genuine bronze figures of ducks and bowl shape ash tray. Felt base. An exquisite piece. Height 3¼ inches. Width of base 5 inches.

BL4085 Nested Ash Tray Set........
Fine quality green alabaster. Four nested ash trays on alabaster base. Genuine bronze art figure. Width 3½ inches. Height 3¼ inches.

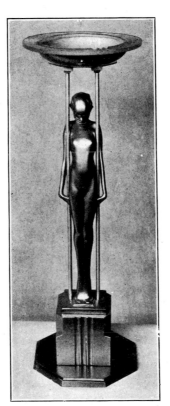

BL4086 Golfer Ash Tray.....................
Realistic action figure of golfer at finish of swing. Figure and base of metal in gun metal finish. Removable ash receptacle, metal base. Height 10¼ inches. Width 7¼ inches.

BL4087 Smoking Stand......
Upright nude figure in silvered black finish supporting two chromium finished rods. Removable frosted crystal ash receiver, 8 inches in diameter. Metal base. Height 23½ inches.

BL4088 Ash Tray, Horse Figure................
BL4089 Ash Tray, Lion Figure.................
Beautiful modern figures, skillfully designed. Gui metal finish spanning jade ash receiver. Metal base

BL3962 Enamel Ash Tray...........
Fine quality book-shaped ash tray, enameled in red and black, gold lined and trimmed. Cigarette rest in lid. Glass lined. Size 3 x 2¼ x ⅞ inches.

BL3963 Enamel Ash Tray...........
Enamel, assorted colors. Size 1½ x 1⅞ x 1½ inches.

BL3964 Enamel Ash Tray Set.................
Genuine hard enamel in black and green. Four individual ash receivers in book shape set in gilt holder as book-case. Each book cover opens having cigarette rest and removable glass receiver. Highly polished. Length 6¼ inches. Height 2¼ inches.

BL3965 Cigarette Box and Ash Tray...........
Black and silver enameled covered box, polished mirror finish cover. Cedar lined cigarette compartment to hold 20 cigarettes. Removable glass lined sliding ash tray with rest. Excellent inexpensive gift. Size 3⅞ x 2 x 7⅞ inches.

BL3966 Ash Tray Nest.................
Black and silver enameled nest and cover with four nested ash trays. Polished nickel trimmings. Height 2½ inches. Diameter 3½ inches.

NOVELTY SILVER ASH RECEIVER
BL3967...........................
Good quality silver plated bowl with novelty figure on removable cover. Removable glass ash tray inside, two cigarette rests. Height 5 inches.

BS5715 Ash Tray.................
Height 6⅞ inches, width 3¼ inches. Removable glass tray with compartment for dumping ashes. Heavily silver plated, ornamented with figure of elephant.

BL3969 Golfer Ash Tray.................
Silver plated figure of golfer, expertly designed. Attached to dump model ash tray. Two cigarette rests, match box holder. Removable top for cleaning. Excellent inexpensive golf prize. Height 4½ inches. Width 4 inches.

BS5717 Smoker's Set...
Consists of large black glass tray, 10 inches long and 4 inches wide, with 4 individual ash trays and cigarette box, holding 50 cigarettes. The box is mounted with police dog, heavily silver plated. Height overall 7¼ inches.

1929 Catalog Page

BL4066 Onyx Tray and Lighter............
Genuine green onyx tray, 5 x 5 x 1½ inches deep.
Large well. Three cigar rests. Equipped with
removable standard lighter which sets in tray.
Can be used on tray or carried in pocket. An
ideal office tray. Special value.

BL4067 Onyx Ash Tray..........
Genuine green onyx tray, two cigar
rests. Artistic figure of cat in genuine
bronze, silver finish. Felt base. Size
4¾ x 3½ inches. Special value.

BL4068 Onyx Ash Tray............
Genuine green onyx tray, three cigar rests.
Genuine bronze figure of Scottie. Felt
base. Size 4¼ x 4¼ x ½ inches.

BL4069 Onyx Ash Tray............................
Genuine green onyx base. Genuine bronze figure of
pointer dog, 3½ inches high. Diameter of tray 7¾
inches.

BL4070 Nested Ash Tray Set.....
Fine quality green alabaster. Four
nested ash trays on alabaster base.
Genuine bronze figure of dog. Height
4 inches. Diameter of base 4 inches.

BL4072 Alabaster Ash Tray, 3 Figures
BL4073 Alabaster Ash Tray, 2 Figures
Fine quality orchid colored alabaster tray and
base. Gold finished art figures. Height 3¼
inches. Exceptional value.

BL4076 Onyx Tray and Lighter.....
Genuine green onyx tray. Equipped with
standard lighter which sets in back; may
be removed for pocket use. Practical inexpensive gift. Size 4¾ x 3¼ inches.

BL4074 Onyx Ash Tray.................
Genuine green onyx, 6 inches, octagonal shape,
deep tray. Genuine bronze figure, 4½ inches
high.

BL4075 Onyx Ash Tray............
Genuine green onyx. 5¾ inch octagonal
tray. Genuine bronze figure of Scottie,
3 inches high. Special value.

BL4078 Onyx Ash Tray...
Genuine green onyx base. Genuine art bronze nude figure, 6 inches high.
10 inch octagonal tray. Splendid wedding gift or trophy.

BL4077 Onyx Ash Tray.................................
Genuine green onyx. Genuine bronze figure, 5 inches long, 2¼
inches high. Tray is 8½ inches long, 5¾ inches deep.

1929 Catalog Page

Silver Plated
SMOKERS' ARTICLES.
Illustrations About One-Half Size.

No. **6581**. Ash Holder with revolving cover .

No. **6577**. Ash Tray, French gray border, length 8½ inches.

No. **6576**. Banjo Ash Receiver, gold lined, ½ size.

No. **6579**. Combination Ash Tray, Cigar Holder, Cutter and Match Holder .

No. **6580**. Ash Receiver, satin, ½ scale.

No. **12**. Cigar cutter, full size ..

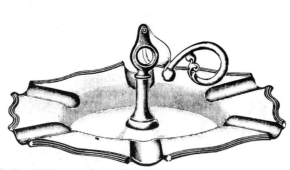

No. **6582**. Ash Tray, Cigar Cutter and Holder.

No. **6583**. Tobacco Jar, gray finish, black inlaid engraving, one-third size.

No. **6578**. Ash Tray and Match Holder, satin engraved, gold lined, illustration two-thirds size

No. **6585**. Cigar Lighter, burnished.

Pepsi Cola Ashtrays

Bakelite Ashtray
Circa 1950's
5" Diameter

Metal Ashtray with
Plastic Bottle Lighter
Circa 1950's
6" Diameter

Tin Ashtray with
Enameled Bottle Cap
Circa 1950's
4" Diameter

Bakelite Ashtray
(Yuba City, CA)
Circa 1950's
6" Diameter

Glass Ashtray
Circa 1950's
6" x 6"

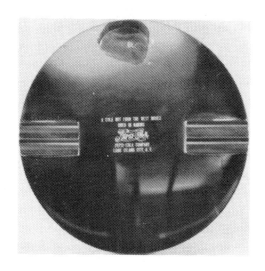

Metal Ashtray
Circa 1950's – 8" Diameter

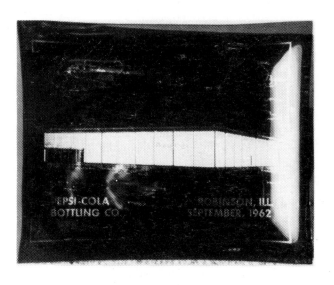

Glass Ashtray (Robinson, IL)
1962 – 10" x 6"

Glass Ashtray
Circa 1970's
4" x 4"

Cigarette Pack
Circa 1970's
2 1/2" x 3 1/2"

Glass Ashtray
Circa 1940's
4" Diameter

Glass Ashtray
Circa 1960's
4" x 4"

Tin Ashtray (Mexican)
Circa 1950's
4" Diameter

Glass Ashtray
(Memphis, MO)
Circa 1950's
4" x 4"

Glass Ashtray
Circa 1960's
4" x 4"

Glass Ashtray
(San Diego, CA)
1963
4" x 4"

No. 00 Advertising Ashtray for R D McKee Hardware
Marked Quality Ware, Erie, PA with a Griswold TM

Advertising Skillet Ashtrays
(left) – No. 00 Marked Griswold Ovens, Fryers,
Ranges Since 1865 with Griswold TM –
(right) – No. 0 Marked Cast Iron Skillet, Erie PA, USA
with Griswold TM –

Advertising Skillet Ashtray
Marked Royal Host Kenmore, NY
3485 Delaware Ave.

Square ashtray with match book holder,
3 1/2" sq. x 1" – p/n 770
circa 1950's

Hearthstone
skillet ashtray
3 1/2" x 1 3/4"
p/n 771
circa 1940's-1950's

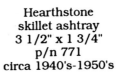

Cowboy Hat Ashtray
5" x 6" x 2 1/4"
marked "Hats off to
Griswold" Erie, PA.
Nickel plated cast iron, circa
1940's

Wind proof ashtray
4 3/8" diameter x 3" tall
p/n 32, small logo
circa 1940's-1950's

Colonial Smoking Set
(Two Views)

1 – p/n 772 marked Griswold
2 – p/n 771 marked with Griswold TM
3 – p/n 773 marked Griswold

1   2   3

Cigarette Cases

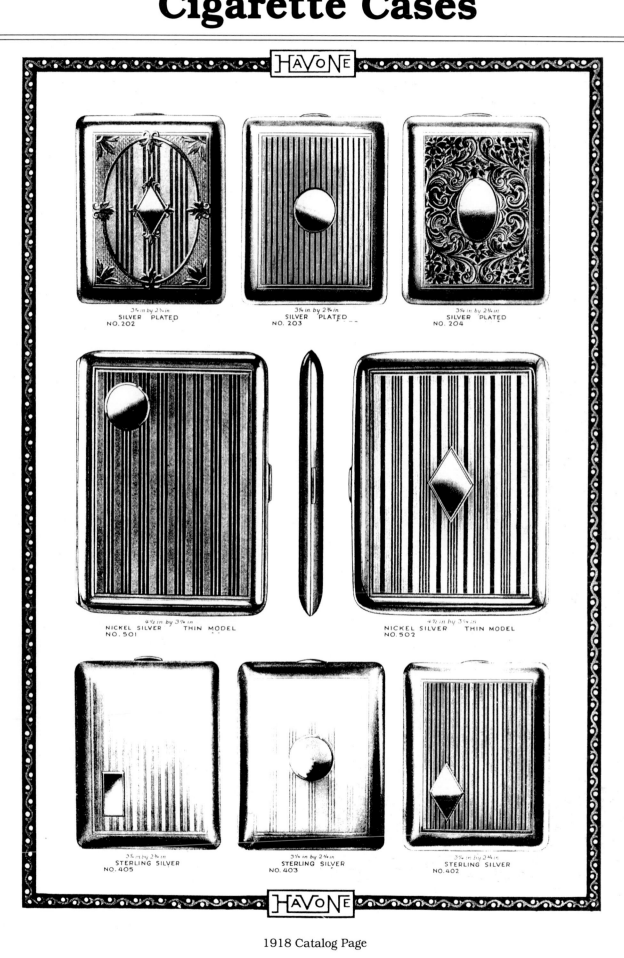

3¼ in by 2¾ in
SILVER PLATED
NO. 202

3¼ in by 2¾ in
SILVER PLATED
NO. 203

3¼ in by 2¾ in
SILVER PLATED
NO. 204

4½ in by 3½ in
NICKEL SILVER   THIN MODEL
NO. 501

4½ in by 3½ in
NICKEL SILVER   THIN MODEL
NO. 502

3¼ in by 2¾ in
STERLING SILVER
NO. 405

3¼ in by 2¾ in
STERLING SILVER
NO. 403

3¼ in by 2¾ in
STERLING SILVER
NO. 402

1918 Catalog Page

HIGHEST GRADE STERLING SILVER AND GERMAN SILVER CIGARETTE CASES

PRICE EACH

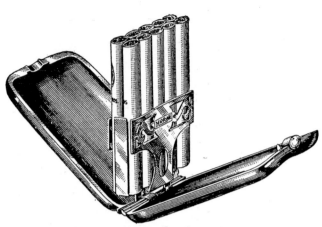

Cut Showing Case Open.

Sterling Silver Havone Cigarette Case. Perfectly Plain Polished, with Stone Set Push Spring Opener. Thin Model, curved to fit the pocket.

Same as above in German Silver, Plain Push Spring Opener.

Sterling Silver Havone Cigarette Case. Handsomely Hand Engraved, with Signet Shield, Stone Set Push Spring Opener, Thin Model, curved to fit the pocket.

Sterling Silver Havone Cigarette Case. Handsomely Hand Engraved, with Plain Center, Stone Set Push Spring Opener. Thin Model, curved to fit the pocket.

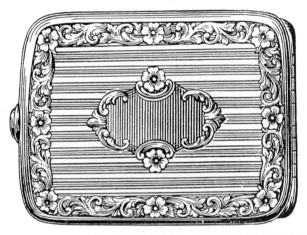

German Silver Havone Cigarette Case, Engraved, with Plain Push Spring Opener. Thin Model, curved to fit the pocket.

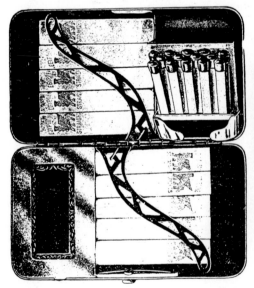

Shows Case Closed.

German Silver Combination Cigarette Case and Match Box. Holds two rows of Cigarettes, Paper of Matches, and place for small coins. Illustration Two-thirds Size.

German Silver Cigarette Case. Thin Model. Holds two rows of Cigarettes. Engraved with Center Shield.

1915 Catalog Page

Indestructible White Finish and Elginite Cigarette Cases

TO HOLD CONVENIENTLY TEN CIGARETTES IN SINGLE ROW—ILLUSTRATIONS FULL SIZE—PRICES EACH

ELGIN AMERICAN MFG. CO. ELGIN. U.S.A.

No. T21301—Elginite straight-line design, medium thin model, chased edge to hold ten cigarettes in single row. Damaskeened gold-lined interior, polished retainer.

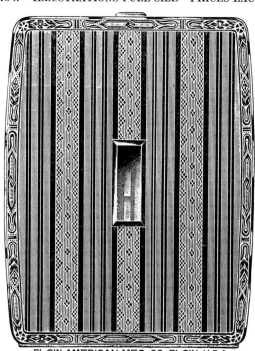

ELGIN AMERICAN MFG. CO. ELGIN. U.S.A.

No. T21302—Elginite straight-line design, medium thin model, chased border, tonneau shape, to hold ten cigarettes in single row. Gold-lined interior, polished retainer.

ELGIN AMERICAN MFG. CO. ELGIN. U.S.A.

No. T21303—Indestructible, white finish, straight-line design, medium thin model, dome edge, to hold ten cigarettes in single row. Damaskeened lined interior, polished bezel and retainer.

ELGIN AMERICAN MFG. CO. ELGIN, U.S.A.

No. T21304—Indestructible white finish, green or yellow enamel front with horse head, Butler back, medium thin model, chased edge, straight sides to hold ten cigarettes in single row. Damaskeened lined interior, polished retainer.

HIGH GRADE GOLD FILLED
CIGARETTE CASES

ILLUSTRATIONS ACTUAL SIZE

Here is extreme "Class!" The very finest
Cigarette Cases obtainable

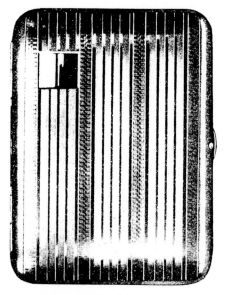

No. 5717 Green Gold Filled
1-Row Swiss Engine Turned and Engraved

No. 5718
White Gold Filled with Green Gold Stripes
Engraved 2-Row

No. 5719 Green Gold Filled
One-Row Figured Design in Red and White Gold

No. 5720 Green Gold Filled
1-Row Straight Line Engraved

No. 5721 White Gold Filled with Green Gold Stripes
1-Row Engraved and Engine Turned

1925 Catalog page

Punch Boards

FOR SOME MIGHTY FAST PROFITS PICK FROM THIS FOURSOME ★ ★ OF DEALS ★ ★

This is

No. 2557

with 42 Winners
1 Pocket Watch
1 Cigarette Case and Lighter
2 Pocket Lighters
2 Pen&Pencil Sets
4 Pen Knives
2 Rings
30 Packs of Cigarettes

This is

No. 2558

with 43 Winners
1 Pocket Watch
1 Necklace
1 Pen&Pencil Set
2 Pencils
2 Animal Pencils
2 Vanity Cases
2 Pen Knives
2 Pocket Lighters
30 Packs of Cigarettes

No. 2557 ONLY...... | Complete with 12 Fine Quality Premiums

These deals take in

Payout 30 cigarette or trade awards @

Show the Big Profit of

Plus Cigarette Profits.

No. 2558 ONLY...... $9.95 List | Complete with 13 Excellent Premiums

This is

No. 2559

42 WINNERS

1 Mantel Clock
1 Pair Binoculars
2 Memo Books
2 Vanity Cases
2 Fountain Pens
2 Rings
2 Pocket Lighters
30 Packs of Cigarettes

This is

No. 2579

40 WINNERS

1 Pocket Watch
1 Cigarette Case and Lighter
2 Skyscraper Lighters
2 Pocket Lighters
2 Sewing Sets
2 Pen Knives
30 Packs of Cigarettes

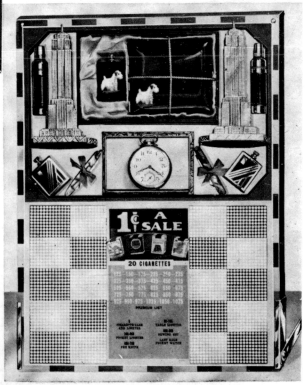

No. 2559 ONLY...... | Complete with 12 High Class Prizes.

No. 2579 ONLY...... | Complete with 10 Wonderful Premiums

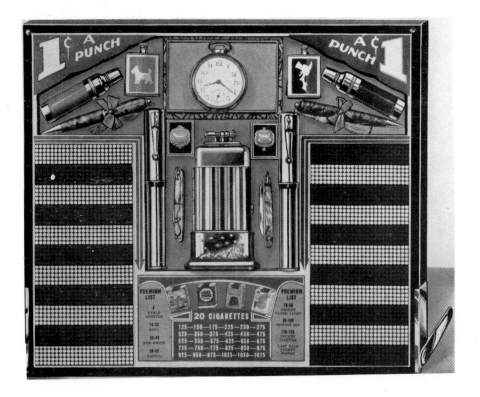

All 1920 Punch Boards

Match Safes

Sterling Silver Match Boxes

Match Box. Heavy Sterling Silver. French Grey Finish. No. **8156**

Match Box. Heavy Sterling Silver. French Grey Finish. No. **8157**

Match Box. Heavy Sterling Silver. French Grey Finish. No. **8158**

Match Box. Heavy Sterling Silver. French Grey Finish. No. **8159**

Match Box. Sterling Silver, French Grey Finish. No. **8160**

Match Box. Sterling Silver, Satin Finish. No. **8161**

Match Box. Sterling Silver, Bright Finish. No. **8162**

Match Box. Sterling Silver, French Grey Finish. No. **8163**

Match Box. Sterling Silver, Bright Finish. No. **8164**

Match Box. Sterling Silver, French Grey Finish. No. **8165**

Match Box. Sterling Silver, Bright Finish. No. **8166**

Match Box. Sterling Silver, Satin Finish No. **8167**

1905 Catalog Page

MATCH SAFES.

Twin, · · · · · ·

ONE DOZEN IN A PACKAGE.

No. 10–Ornamental iron, copper bronzed, self-closing, · · · ·

HALF DOZEN IN A BOX.

Square, small, length 3 in., · ·
Square, large, length 3½ in., · ·

ONE DOZEN IN A PACKAGE.

Round, length 4 in., · · ·

ONE DOZEN IN A PACKAGE.

Adamantine, Bronzed, Self Closing.

No.		6	7
Inches,	·	3¾×1¾×1⅜	5×2¼×1⅝
Per dozen	·		

NO. 6, ONE THIRD DOZEN; NO. 7, ONE SIXTH DOZEN IN A BOX.

1899 Catalog Page

POCKET MATCH SAFES.

No. 6.   No. 9.   No. 90.   No. 5.

No. 6–Charm, nickel plated,   ·   ·   ·   ·   ·   ·   ·   ·   ·   ·   per dozen

No. 9–Excelsior, nickel plated,   ·   ·   ·   ·   ·   ·   ·   ·   "

No. 90–Excelsior, nickel plated, body leather covered,   ·   ·   ·   ·   "

No. 5–Automatic, nickel plated,   ·   ·   ·   ·   ·   ·   ·   ·   "

ONE DOZEN IN A BOX.

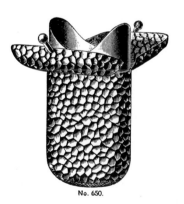

No. 65.   No. 650.   No. 7.

No. 65–Mascot, plain, nickel plated,   ·   ·   ·   ·   ·   ·   ·   ·

No. 650–Mascot, decorated, nickel plated,   ·   ·   ·   ·   ·   ·

No. 7–Combination safe and cigar cutter, nickel plated,   ·   ·   ·   ·

ONE DOZEN IN A BOX.

1899 Catalog Page

STERLING SILVER MATCH BOXES.

Shown Full Size.

No. **5860.** Raised figure, French gray, gold lined, extra heavy

No. **5859.** Raised Indian head

No. **5862.** The Elk Match Safe, heavy embossed design

No. **5863.** Embossed, gray finish

No. **5870.** Polished, embossed

No. **5864.** Plain polished, beaded, gold lined

No. **5868.** Polished, raised embossed border, gold lined

No. **5861.** Raised figure, French gray

No. **5869.** Satin finished, embossed

No. **5866.** Raised border, French gray, gold lined

No. **5867.** Burnished, raised border, gold lined

No. **5865.** Embossed, French gray finish

1905 Catalog Page

Sterling Silver

7336. **Shrine Match Box,** French Gray Finish.

7339. French Gray Finish.

7338. Bright Polished and Engraved.

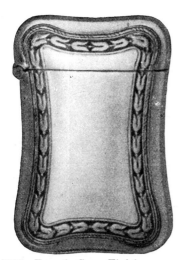

7340. French Gray Finish.

7341. Bright Engraved.

7342. French Gray Finish.

7344. French Gray Finish.

7345. French Gray Finish.

7346. French Gray Finish.

1906 Catalog Page

STERLING SILVER MATCH SAFES (925/1000 Fine)

No. 563001, Price, French Gray Finish.

No. 563002, Price, French Gray Finish.

No. 563003, Price, French Gray Finish.

No. 563004, Price, French Gray Finish.

No. 563005, Price, French Gray Finish.

No. 563006, Price, French Gray Finish.

No. 563007, Price, French Gray Finish.

No. 563008, Price, French Gray Finish.

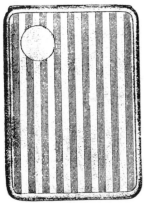

No. 563009, Price, Sterling Silver Match Box.

No. 563010, Price, Sterling Silver Match Box.

No. 563011, Price, Polished Finish.

No. 563012, Price, Polished Finish.

1915 Catalog Page

STERLING SILVER PATENT MATCH BOXES, CIGAR CUTTERS, CIGARETTE HOLDERS, STAMP BOXES, PENCILS AND FILES

Match Boxes are Flat, Made to Hold Paper Safety Matches. All Made with Extra Ring to Fasten on Waldemar Chain.

No. 817201,
Sterling Silver Match Box for Paper Safety Matches.
Engraved.

No. 817202,
Sterling Silver Match Box for Paper Safety Matches.
Hand Engraved.

No. 817203,
Sterling Silver Match Box for Paper Safety Matches.
Hammered Design.
No. 817204,
Same as above in Nickel Silver.

No. 817205,
Sterling Silver Match Box for Paper Safety Matches.
Engraved.

No. 817210,
Sterling Silver Match Box for Patent Paper Safety Matches.
Perfectly Plain.

No. 563204,
Cigar Cutter.
Solid Gold.
Perfectly Plain.
No. 563204½,
Sterling Silver.
Perfectly Plain.

No. 563205,
Cigar Cutter.
Solid Gold.
Engraved.
No. 563205½,
Sterling Silver.
Engraved.

No. 563206, Match Box.
Highest Grade. Gold Filled. Plain.
Made to hold a card of Paper Matches.
With Loop to fasten to Waldemar Chain.
No. 563206½,
Same as above in Solid Gold.

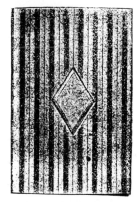

No. 860304,
Safety Matchbox Holder.
Engine Turned Design.

No. 860305,
Safety Matchbox Holder.
Perfectly Plain.

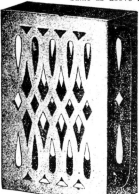

No. 860307,
Safety Matchbox Holder.
For the Smoking Table.

No. 860308,
Sterling Silver Cigarette Holder with Mouth Piece. Plain Polished.

No. 860303, Sterling Silver Cigarette Paper Holder,
Fancy Engraved. Will Hold Regulation Size Papers.

1918 Catalog Page

41

STERLING SILVER AND SOLID GOLD MATCH SAFES (925/1000 Fine)

See Page 603 for Other Sterling Match Safes.

No. 860201, Price,
French Gray Finish.

No. 860202, Price,
French Gray Finish.

No. 860203, Price,
French Gray Finish.

No. 860204, Price, $4.50
Polished Finish.

Solid Gold Match Box.
No. 860205,
Plain Roman.
Heavy.
No. 860206,
Same as above with
Genuine Cut Diamond.

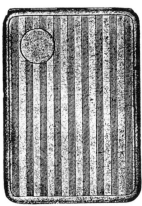

No. 860207, Price,
French Gray Finish.

No. 860208, Price,
French Gray Finish.

No. 860209, Price,
Sterling Silver Match Box.
Made to hold a Card of
Paper Matches
No. 860210, Price,
Same as above in Solid Gold.

No. 860211, Price,
French Gray Finish.

NICKEL SILVER MATCH SAFES

PRICE EACH

No. 860212,
Nickel Silver Match Safe for
Paper Matches. Regulation Size.
Hammered Design.

No. 860213, Match Safe,
Nickel Silver.

No. 860214, Match Box,
Nickel Silver. Made to take a
card of Paper Matches.

No. 860215, Match Box,
Nickel Silver. Made to take a
card of Paper Matches.

1918 Catalog Page

GERMAN SILVER MATCH SAFES, CIGARETTE CASE AND STERLING SILVER CIGARETTE CASE, CIGAR CASE AND SPECTACLE CASES

No. 562801, Match Safe.
German Silver.

No. 562802, Match Safe.
German Silver.

No. 562803, Match Safe.
German Silver.

No. 562804, Match Box,
German Silver.
Made to take a card of
Paper Matches.

No. 566006,
Match Holder and Ash Tray.
Art Noveaux, Green and Gilt Finish.
Head in Blue, Black and Red.

Match Boxes

Jap Match Box

S8809   S8807

S8809— Match Box—
Round shape, 2¾ inches
long, gun metal finish. 1
doz. in box.

J8825— Jap Match Box.
1¾ x 2⅜ in., metal, b l a c k
Japanned, finish gold and
silver, oriental design, contains match striker, automatic clasps. 1 doz. in box.

No. 566007,
Match Holder and Ash Tray.
Art Noveaux, Green and Gilt
Finish.

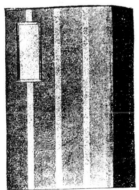

No. 561605, Each,
Sterling Silver Match Box Holder.
Will Hold Full Box of Safety Matches.
Engine Turned.

S8808—Match Box—1½ x
2¾ in. Gilt finish, spring
cover. 1 doz. in box.

No. 566009,
Match Holder.
Antique Copper.

No. 566011,
Match Holder.
Art Noveaux, Blue, Green and
Gilt Finish.

No. 566012,
Match Box Holder.
Antique Brass.

C.C. 5782

C.C. 5782. Silveroid Match Case,

MH-48 Ceresota Flour Tin
3½" x 5"

MH-61 Laurel Stoves &
Ranges Tin 3½" x 5"

MH-75 Tenorio Cigar Cardboard
6½" x 8½"

MH-47 Bull Dog Cut Plug
Tin 3½" x 6½"

MH-9—BORN RANGE
Tin Match Holder
Size 3½ x 5 Inches

MH-51 Columbia
Mill Co. Tin
2¼" x 5½"

MH-1—ABC BREAD
Size 3¼ x 5 Inches

MH-2—AGATE FLOOR FINISH
Tin Match Holder
Size 3¾ x 6¾ Inches

44

SILVER PLATED WARE.

CIGAR HOLDER AND ASH RECEIVER (Cut Actual Size)
Sterling Silver, polished; gold lined receiver.
No. T207   Each.

Smoking Set.   Burnished, Gold Lined.   Half size
No. 8851

No. 6584.   Cigar Lamp, burnished.

No. 6546.   Match Holder
satin engraved, gold lined.
½ size .

Smoker's Lamp.   Plain Burnished.
No. 8856 .

No. 6542.   Match Holder, satin
engraved, gold lined, ½
size

No. 6543.   Match Holder, 3
handles, satin engraved,
gold lined, ½ size .

Smoking Set.   Embossed Burnished.
No. 8850 .

No. 6549.   Match Holder,
satin, gilt lined, ½ scale.

Advertising

January 28, 1939 Magazine Ad

1929 Magazine Ad

1939 Magazine Ad

1942 Magazine Ad

1942 Magazine Wartime Ad

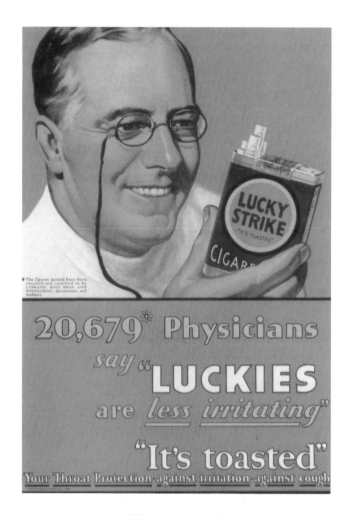

1930 Magazine Ad

1930 Magazine Ad

1944 Magazine Ad

1945 Magazine Ad

1943 Magazine Ad

1942 Magazine Ad

1955 Magazine Ad

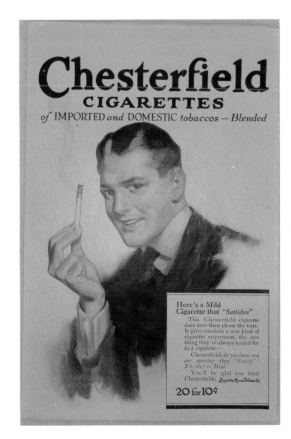

1917 Magazine Ad

1928 Magazine Ad

THEY CERTAINLY DO KNOW THEIR
CIGARETTES, THIS YOUNGER CROWD!

SOMETHING ABOUT FATIMA—
ITS GREATER DELICACY, ITS
MORE SKILLFUL BLENDING
OF FLAVORS — HAS MADE IT,
AS IN OTHER DAYS, A CON-
SPICUOUS FAVORITE WITH
THE YOUNGER SET.

FATIMA

OUTSTANDING FAVORITE AMONG HIGHER - PRICED CIGARETTES !

1928 Magazine Ad

1916 Magazine Ad

1919 Magazine Ad

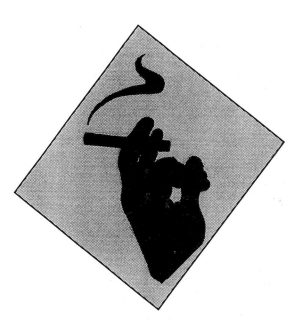

1918 Magazine Ad

1917 Magazine Ad

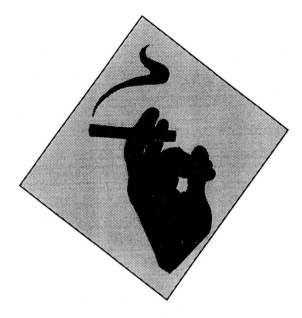

1920 Magazine Ad

1916 Catalog Ad

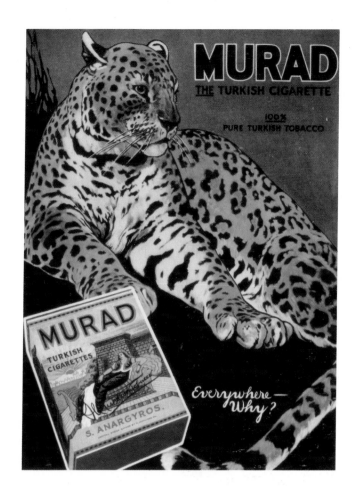

1914 Catalog Ad

1918 Catalog Ad

1915 Magazine Ad

1914 Magazine Ad

Advertising Items

Framed Fatima Tin Sign,
26" x 38"

Piedmont Cigarette Advertising Chair

Kool Advertising Mat
9$^{1/2}$" x 7$^{1/2}$" x $^{5/16}$"

1930's Porcelain Enameled Sign 20" x 4"

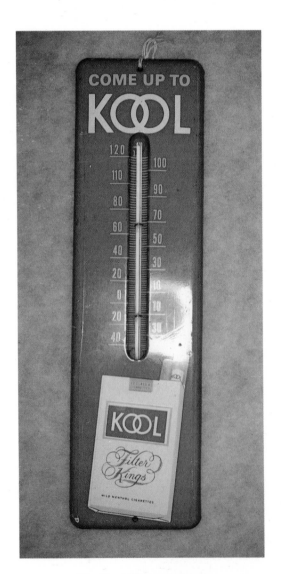

Tin Kool Thermometer

Tin Marvels Thermometer, 12" x 4"

Paper Cigarette Advertising Sign
12" x 24"

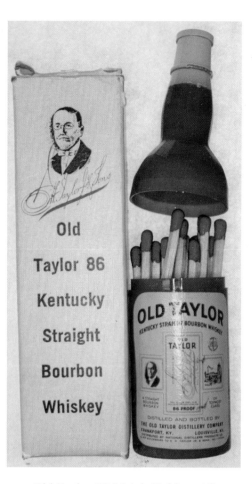

Old Taylor 86 Match Holder with
Original Box, 1" x 4"

Black Cat Cardboard Advertising Sign

Cardboard Advertising Camel Cigarette Box,
2¹/₈" x 2⁷/₈" x ⁷/₈"

Cardboard Advertising Sign
18" x 12"

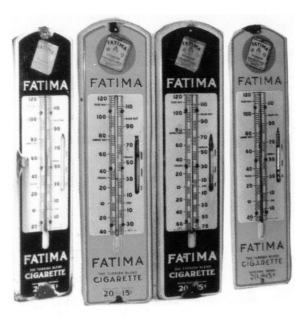

All Porcelain
7" x 27"

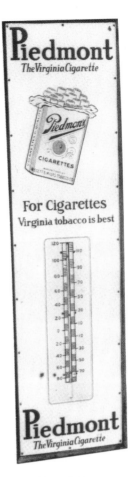

Porcelain
21" x 27"

Postcard

Framed Trolley Car Card, Cardboard
11" x 21"

Framed Cardboard
32" x 47"

Porcelain
36" x 11"

1940 Camel Flyer, Front and Back, 4¹/²" x 7" (Closed)

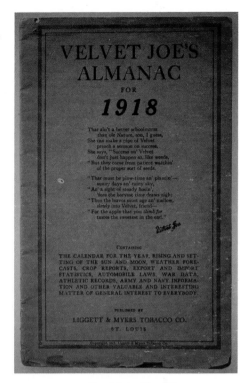

Booklet, 8" x 5"

Camel Flyer, Front and Back, 4¹/²" x 7 (closed), 1940's

34 Page Catalog, 8¹/⁴" x 6"

Kool Presidential Election Pamphlet, 1964

61

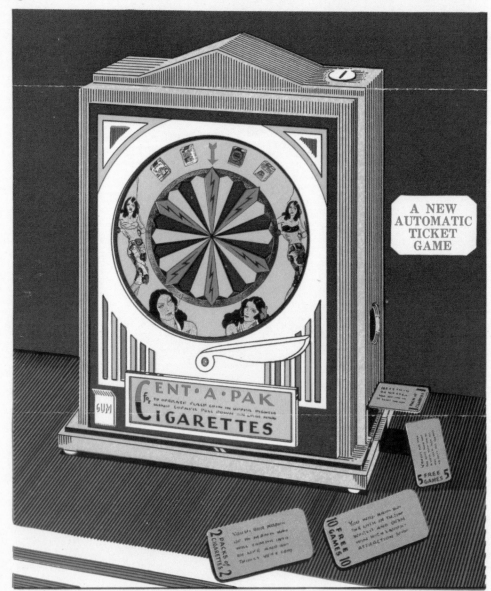
Paper Flier, Circa 1930's

Kool Composition Figure
About 4" Tall

Famous Old Gold Girl Advertising Item
8¹/₂" High

Lark Cigarette Advertising
Wind-Up Toy, Made in Japan,
2" x 3³/₄"

Evans Trig-A-Lite Lighter with
Lucky Strike Green
Advertising,
1¹/₂" x ¹/₂" x 2"

World Fair Items

Enamel Ware, 5^{1/2}"

Century of Progress Items, Top-Cigarette Case 1933, 6^{1/2}" x 3^{1/4}", Middle 1934, 2^{1/4}" x 1^{1/2}" x ^{3/4}", Bottom- 1934, (On the bottom it reads: This souvenir contains sand taken from Lake Michigan. at the World's Fair Grounds. A real Souvenir of a Century of Progress Exposition.) 3^{1/8}" x 1"

1993 Chicago World's Fair Ashtray, 5^{1/4}" x 5^{1/4}"

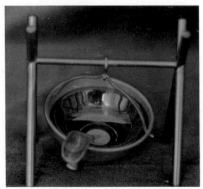

Hanging Copper Ashtray Advertising 1934 A Century of Progress Chicago Glass Insert in Pot. 4^{1/4}" x 4^{1/4}" x 3^{3/4}"

1931 Ashtray, New York World's Fair Unisphere, 3^{1/2}" x 3^{1/2}"

Punch Boards

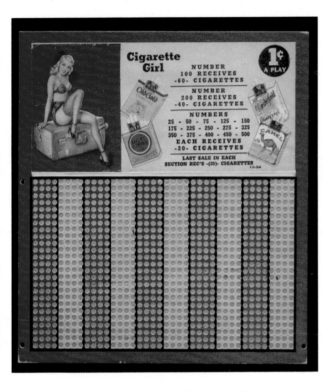

1929 Punchboard, 10" x 11"

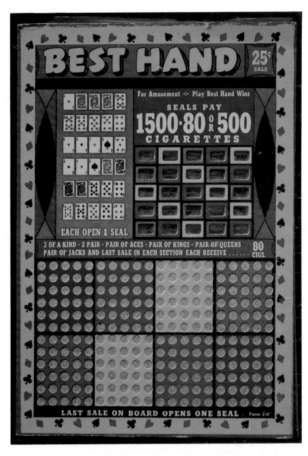

Best Hand 1950 Punch Board,
8" x 11"

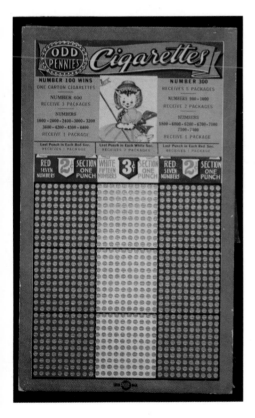

Early 1930's Punch Board,
6³/₄" x 11"

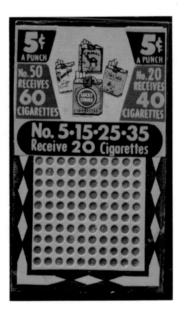

1930's Punch Board
2¹/₂" x 4¹/₄"

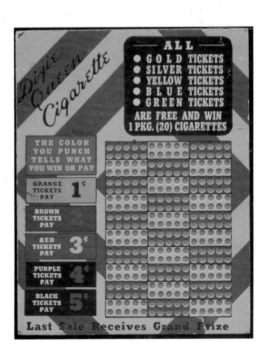

Early 1930's Punch Board
8" x 10"

1930's Punch Board with Cigarette Advertising
8" x 3/4" x 8 1/2"

Punch Board with Cigarette Advertising
8" x 3/4" x 8 1/2"

Punch Board with Cigarette Advertising
8" x 3/4" x 8 1/2"

1930's Punch Board
9 1/2" x 9 1/2"

1940's Punch Board
9" x 9³/₄"

1940's-1950's Punch Board
10¹/₂" x 10¹/₂"

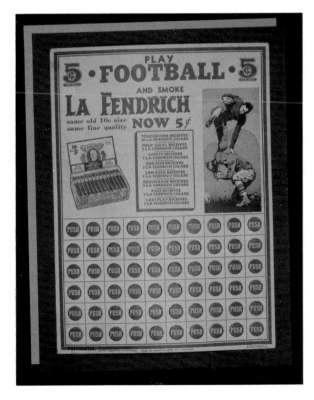

1934 Punch Board
7" x 9"

1940's Super Smokes Punch Board
13" x 13"

Playing Cards

Playing Cards

Standard Size Decks

Standard Size Decks

Cigarette Advertising Playing Cards

Cigarette Advertising Playing Cards

Two Packs of Harley-Davidson Cigarettes
with Free Playing Cards, 5³/₄" x 8¹/₂"

Candy Cigarette and Cigar Packs

Assortment of Candy Cigarettes,
All Above are 3¹/⁴" x 2¹/⁸",
Except Roll Gold, 2⁷/⁸" x 2¹/⁴"

Candy Cigars by Four Star Candy Co.
of Newark NJ, All 2¹/⁴" x ¹/²" x 4¹/⁴"

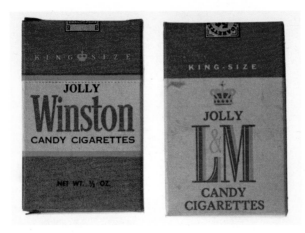

Candy Cigarettes by Four Star Candy Co.
of Newark, NJ, Both 3" x 2" x ³/⁴"

Candy Cigarettes by Four
Star Candy Co. of
Newark, NJ, 3" x 2" x ³/⁴"

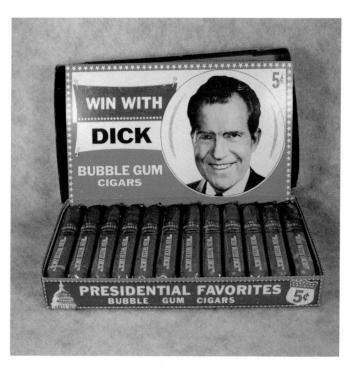

"Win With Dick" Display of Bubble Gum Cigars

"Win With H.H.H" Display of Bubble Gum Cigars

Lucky Strike Candy Cigarettes,
Battle Ship on Back

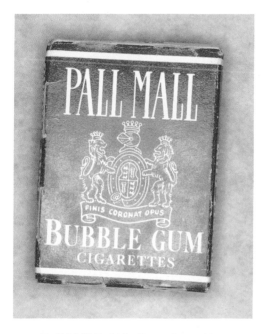

Pall Mall Bubble Gum Cigarettes

Assorted Tobacco Silks

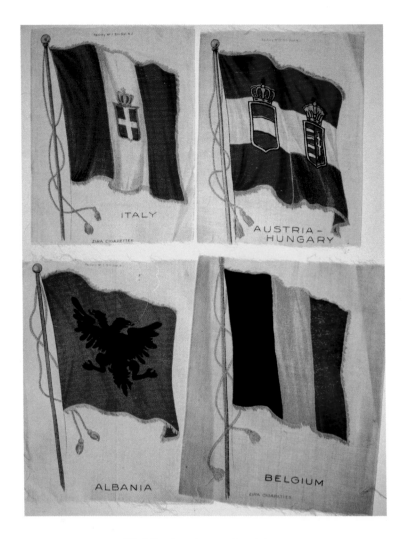

All Silks Are Approximately
5 x 7 Inches Square

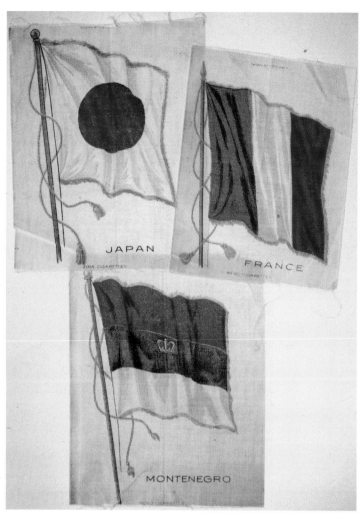

All Silks Are Approximately
5 x 7 Inches Square

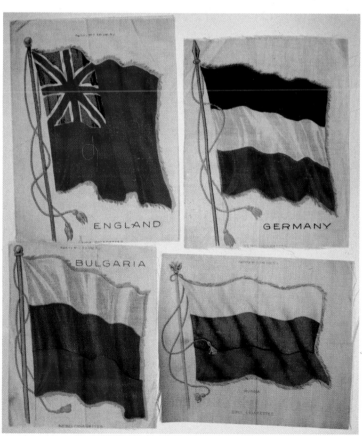

Sheet Music

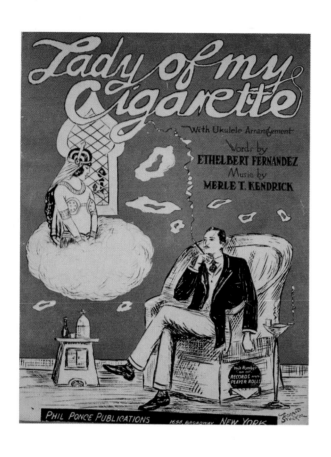

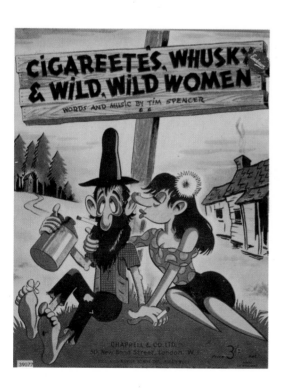

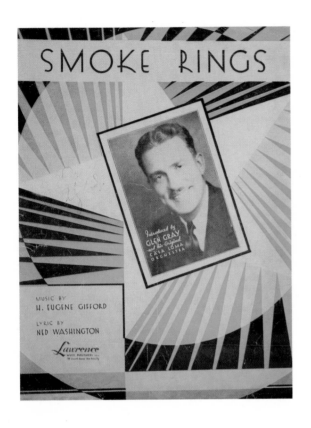

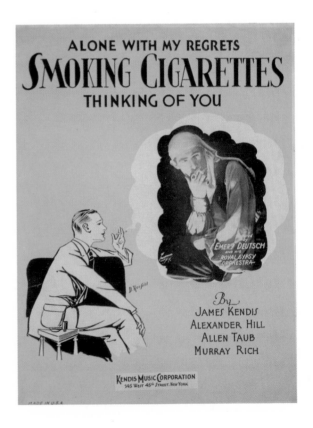

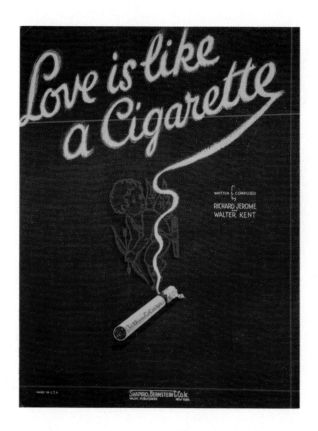

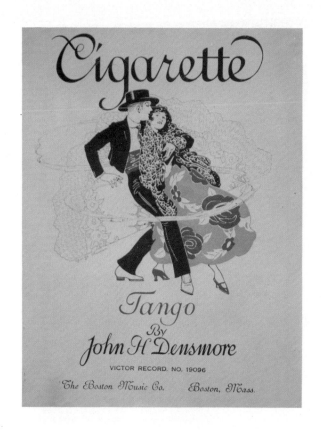

Match Boxes

Assortment of Match Boxes

Match Boxes
1 1/2" x 1 x 3/8"

Assortment of Standard Size Matches

Match Boxes, Pall Mall is 1 3/4" x 2 1/2",
All Others are Proportionately Sized

Top-Satin Tip Matches from Universal Match
Corporation, 10 boxes, 7" x 2³/₈" x 1¹/₂";
Middle-Camel Matches, 50 Books,
6¹/₂" x 4" x 1¹/₂"; Bottom-Vest Pocket Safety
Matches Made in Sweeden, 12 Boxes,
5¹/₈" x 2¹/₄" x 7/₈"

Top Left-Matches 1¹/₄" x 2¹/₄";
Top Right-Matches 2³/₄" x 1³/₄"; Middle Left-
Set of Matches, Made in Italy, Each
1¹/₄" x 2"; Bottom Left-Matches 2¹/₄" x 1¹/₄";
Bottom Right-Match Box Made in Sweeden,
2¹/₂" x 4¹/₄"

Match Box and Trivet
4" x 4" x 1"

Composition and Glass
4¹/₄" x 4¹/₄" x 7/₈"

Top-Birds Eye Diamond
Matches, 4³/₄" x 2³/₄" x 1³/₄";
Middle-American Swan Diamond
Matches 5" x 2¹/₂" x 1¹/₂";
Bottom-Oriental Box Matches,
Made in Japan, 4¹/₂" x 3" x ³/₄"

Marlboro Display with Match Boxes
that are Flip-Top Like the Cigarettes
1991, 12" x 3" x 5¹/₂"

Diamond Matches, 6 Boxes, 11" x 5" x 2³/₄"

Back

American Ace Matches
5" x 2⁵/₈" x 1¹/₂"

Match Holders

Cast Iron Wall Matchholder with Striker
"Turn off burner when not using." "Matches are
cheaper than gas" Pat, June 13, 1899

Cast Iron Wall Match Holder with Hand Painting
3¹/₄" x 4¹/₄"

Cast Iron Wall Match Holder, 3³/₈" x 7¹/₄"

Tin Wall Match Holder, 3" x 6¹/₈"

Fish and Cowboy Boot Wall Match Holder

Brass Wall Match Holder

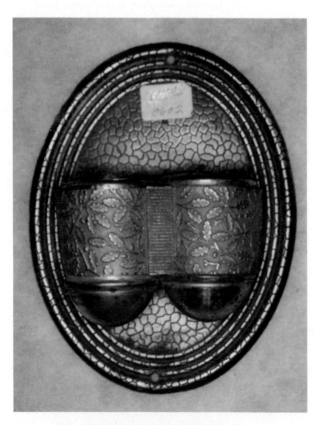

Tin Wall Match Holder

Tin Wall Match Holder

Match Book Dispenser

Cast Iron Wall (Kitchen) Match
Box Holder with Striker on side,
4" x 7$^{1/2}$"

Match Safe with Cigar Cutter
on Bottom

Matchcover Holders
Top Left-Art Deco, Metal,
Top Right-Bakelite, Middle Left-Metal
Middle Right, Aluminum
Bottom-Double Sided Plastic

Match Box Holders,
SPECIAL HOLDERS: Top Right-WWI
Copper, Middle Left-WW1 Brass

Advertising Match Safes Both 2³/₄" x 1¹/₂"

Match Safes
Left-2¹/₂" Right-3"

Back

Match Box Holder
Cigar Cutter USA
2¹/₄" x 3¹/₈" x ³/₄"

Top Left- Marbles Match Safe 2¹/₂",
Top Right-Match Safe 2¹/₂",
Middle Left-Schlitz Match Safe
1¹/₂" x 2¹/₂", Middle Right-Made in
Italy 1¹/₄" x 2¹/₄", Botom-1" x 1¹/₂"

Match Box
Covers
Top 1" x 1¹/²"
Bottom-
Denmark,
1" x 1³/⁴"

MATCH BOX HOLDERS

Top Left- Gay Paris

Top Right- Made in Italy- Porcelain

Mid. Left- Metal on top and bottom

Mid. Right- Hand Chased

Bottom Left- Doskow Silver Plate

Bottom Right- Match Safe, Great
  "Hunters" Litho by Bryan and May
  with striker.

Sterling Silver Match and
Candle Holder
2" x 3¹/²" x 1¹/²"

Glass and Metal
Match Holder and
Ashtray Set,
Ashtray:
2⁷/⁸" x 1⁷/⁸"
Match Holder:
1¹¹/¹⁶" x 1¹/⁸" x ⁵/⁸"

1870 Cast Iron
Wall Match Holder
7¹/²" x 3¹/²" x 1¹/²"

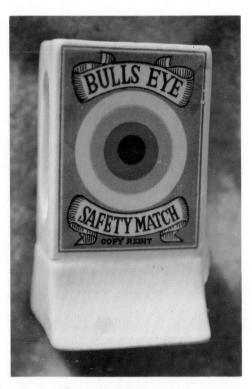

English Match Box Holder
Picture is Actual Size

Brass Match Holder
with Dog Face On
Each Side.
$2^{1/8}$" x 3"

Porcelain Wall Match Holder with
Strikers on Sides
$4^{1/2}$" x $2^{1/4}$" x $1^{1/4}$"

Top Left-Cloisonne Match Box Cover $1^{1/2}$" x $2^{1/4}$"
Top Right- Match Box Cover $1^{1/2}$" x $2^{1/4}$"
Bottom-Brass Match Box Holder $2^{1/2}$" x $2^{3/4}$"

King Tut or Egyptian Match Holder
(Cast Bronze) #2826

Match Holders with Striker

Advertising Foreign Match Holder with Striker Around Top of Base, 3$^{1/4}$" x 3$^{1/4}$"

Porcelain Match Holder and Ashtray with Striker Around Top of Match Holder, By Cook Ceramic Mfg. Co. Trenton NJ, Custom Made for Keen's English Chop House, 5$^{3/4}$" x 4"

Advertising Foreign Match Holder with Striker Edge Around Top, 3$^{1/2}$" x 3$^{3/4}$"

Match Holder with Striker on Side Made in Austria

Porcelain Match Holder O.P Co. Syracuse, China #H-3, 5$^{1/2}$" x 3$^{3/8}$"

Match Holder with Striker, Match Striker ©Lawson and Lawson Inc., 2$^{1/2}$" x 2$^{1/8}$"

Brass Match Holder, 4$^{1/2}$" x 1$^{7/8}$" x 3$^{1/4}$"

Ashtray and Match Holder, 3$^{1/2}$" x 4$^{1/2}$"

Cigarette and Match Holder with Striker, Gibson Girl Motif,
8" x 3¹/⁴"

Porcelain Striker and Ashtray,
Japanese, Height 3" x 3³/⁴"

Match Holder Marked "Brands
Famous Stoves•Ranges &
Furnaces, Brand Stove Co.
Milwaukee

Match Holder and Striker, 6" x 4"

Small Ashtray with Match Striker,
3³/⁴" x 2¹/²"

Match Box Holder, England, 4¹/⁴" x 3"

Advertising Match Holder and
Ashtray, Striker's on Side of
Match Holder, 5" x 2¹/²"

Match Striker/Ashtray and Cigarette Holder combo.
Eldorado-Made in Belgium Brevet SGDG 6" x 5$^{4/8}$"
(closed view) **Item Courtesy of Renee Martin**
(three views pictured on this page)

When a match is pulled out of the holder
it automaticaly lights.
(open view)

This view shows how the ashtrays come
off the post in the middle.
(open view)

Match Holders with Ashtray

Brass Ashtray and Match Holder,
USA, 4" x 5"

Brass and Glass Ashtray with Match
Holder and Candle Holder, 6$^{1/2}$" x 5$^{1/2}$"

Brass Korea Ashtray and
Cigarette Holder,
6$^{1/4}$" x 3$^{1/4}$" x 3"

Ashtray with Match
Holder, Bechard Mfg. Co.
Chicago, 4$^{1/2}$" x 3"

Ashtray and Matchholder
4$^{5/8}$" x 2$^{1/2}$"

Brass Match Holder
4" x 1$^{3/4}$"

Faberware Brass Ashtray with Match Holder,
6$^{1/4}$" x 3$^{3/4}$"

Copper Ashtray with Match Holder
Patent Jan. 16, 1917, 3$^{1/8}$"

90

Plated metal match box holder and ashtray.
Advertising Quincy Shaft House.

Silver Ashtray and Match Holder,
Made in Argentina.
3" x 5$^{1/2}$"

Bronze Art Noveau
match holder & ashtray
by Fank and Dekeyser, New York
Patented Nov. 10, 1986

Match Holder, Art Deco, Black Finish
10$^{1/4}$" x 2$^{1/4}$" x 3"

Match Box Holder, Cast Brass-
Ashtray, Rothschild Brothers, USA
5$^{1/4}$" x 3" x 4"

Early Brass Match Holder and
Ashtray – 4" x 3$^{1/2}$"

Milk Glass Match Holder, 3⁷/₈" x 2¹/₈" x 2"

Ashtray and Match Holder Composition,
6³/₄" x 4"

Match Holder and Ashtray Advertising
Gold Seal Champagne

Carnival Glass Ashtray with
Match Holder, 5⁵/₈" x 1¹/₄"

Glass Ashtray with Match
Holder, 5" x 2"

Ashtray and Match Book Holder
New York City Bristol Hotel,
Pat'd May 31, 1921, 3¹/₄" x 3¹/₂"

Hall China Ashtray with Match Holder
Property of Palmer House, Chicago,
$3^{3/4}$" x $5^{1/2}$"

Advertising Ashtray and Match Holder Made
in Germany, $4^{7/8}$" x $3^{3/4}$" x $2^{7/8}$"

Advertising Ashtray with Match Holders
Cast Iron Bottom (Enameled), Water
Fountain on Top EBCO Mfg. Co.,
$8^{1/4}$" x $5^{1/2}$" x $5^{7/8}$"

Fatima Cigarette Holder,
Very Hard to Find, $3^{3/4}$" x $5^{1/4}$" x 6"

Enameled Cast Iron Ashtray and Match Holder
Advertising a Lavatory Co., $5^{3/4}$" x 4"

Match Holder and Ashtray Set, Iron Stone China by
Mason's of England, Fruit Basket Design.
"Guaranteed Permanent Acid Resisting Colours."
Ashtray $3^{1/2}$" x $3^{1/2}$", Match Holder $2^{1/2}$" x 2" x $1^{1/8}$"

93

Cigarette Pack and Match Holders

Brass Ashtray and Cigarette Pack
Holder, Oriental Man Made in
Korea, 5$^{1/4}$" x 4$^{1/4}$"

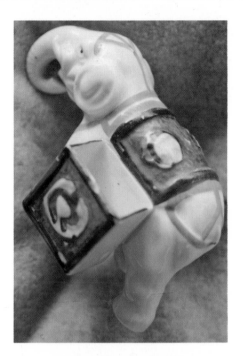

Japan Match Box Holder,
3$^{3/4}$" x 4$^{3/4}$" x 6$^{1/2}$"

Wall Pocket Ashtray and
Cigarette Pack Holder
Advertising Chicago -
Buckingham Fountain,
3" x 4$^{3/4}$"

Nippon Ashtray with Cigarette and Match
Holders with transitional marking on bottom.
4$^{1/4}$" x 4$^{3/4}$" x 5$^{5/8}$"

Noritake Cigarette
Pack Holder, Hand
Painted in Japan,
4$^{3/4}$" x 2$^{3/8}$"

Elephant Ashtray and Match Holder Hand
Painted in Japan, 4$^{1/2}$" x 6$^{1/2}$" x 4"

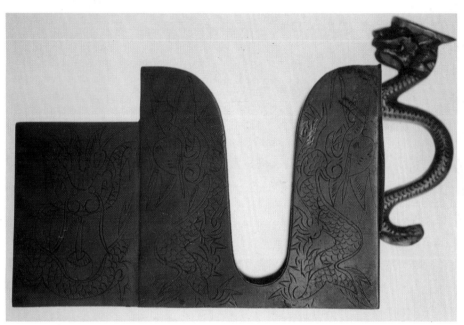

Brass Oriental Match Holder & Cigarette Pack Holder, Made in China,
5$^{1/2}$" x $^{7/8}$" x 3$^{3/4}$"

Front   Back

Fatima Turkish Cigarette Holder and Calendar, 5$^{1/2}$" x 4$^{1/4}$"

Cigarette Rollers

King Cigarette Maker with Original Box, with Six
Original Cigarette Makers, 6⁷/₈" x ³/₄" x ³/₄"

Top Cigarette Rolling Combination,
3" x 4¹/₂"

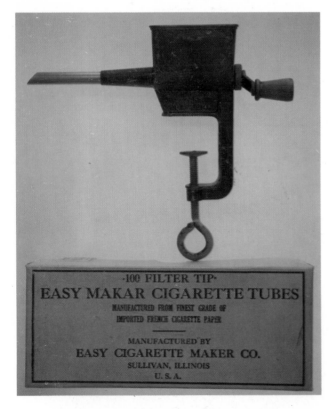

Target Junior Cigarette Rolling Machine, 6⁵/₈" x 3¹/₄"

Easy Cigarette Maker Co. Sullivan, IL 5⁷/₈" x 6³/₄" x 2⁵/₈"
Filter Tip Easy Maker Cigarette Tubes in Original
1933 Box, 7¹/₄" x 3" x 1⁵/₈"

Assortment of Cigarette Rolling Papers,
Normal Size

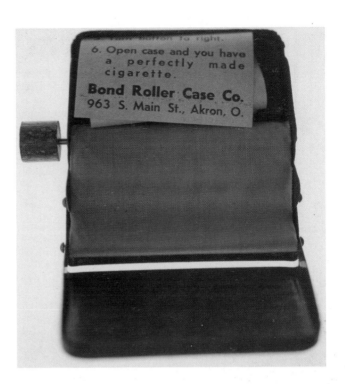

Cigarette Rolling Machine by Bond Roller Case Co.
Akron, OH 1943, Open 2⁵/₈" x 3¹/₈"

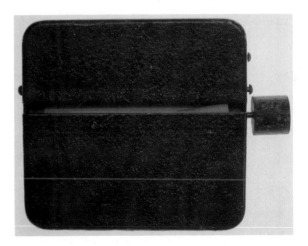

Closed Cigarette Rolling Machine Shown Above

Metal Cigarette Paper
Dispenser

Cigarette Roller, 6" x 3" x 2¹/₂"

Cigarette Novelties

Kent Cigarette Advertising Squirt Gun,
2" x 3$^{1/8}$"

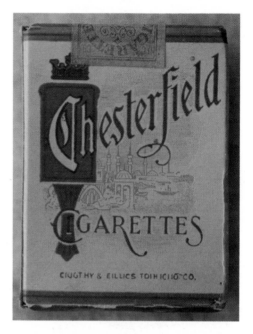

Chesterfield Advertising Trick Cigarette
Pack by J. Cheint Co., 2$^{1/8}$" x 2$^{7/8}$" x $^{3/4}$"

Back Side of Chesterfield
Trick Cigarette Pack

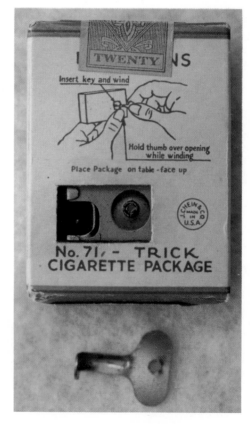

Cigarette Dispensers

Cigarette Holder and Dispenser (Open)
4" x 5¹/²"

Closed

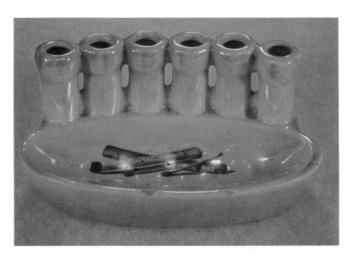

Ashtray and Cigarette Holder, Austrian
5¹/⁸" x 3" x 2¹/⁴"

Musical Cigarette Box, Made in Italy

Cast Iron Cigarette Dispenser, Ciga Rola,
Model A #4, 6" x 4$^{1/4}$" x 2$^{3/4}$"

Made in Korea Cigarette Holder (Open)

Tin Cigarette Dispenser, Cigarette Comes Out of
Rear End, 10$^{1/4}$" x 9"

Cigarette Holder and Dispenser by Park Sherman
7$^{1/2}$" x 4"

Cigarette Dispenser, Made in Occupied Japan,
2$^{1/2}$" x 4"

Carved Wood Cigarette Dispenser,
8" x 5" x 5"

Cigarette Dispenser, Napco, Inc.,
6" x 3"

Large Store Model Cigarette Dispenser
15" x 8¹/₂"

Keystone Cigarette Dispenser "Dispendador" by the
Norlipp Co. of Chicago, 3¹/₄" x 5" x 4¹/₄"

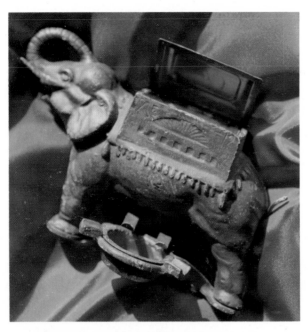

Cigarette Dispenser, Circa 1910, Cast Iron,
8$^{1/2}$" x 4$^{1/2}$" x 4"

Cigarette Dispenser, Plastic USA, 6$^{1/2}$" x 4" x 3$^{1/2}$"

Enameled Metal Cigarette Box, 3$^{1/4}$" x 6"

Pot Metal-Plated 5$^{3/4}$" x 4"

Art Deco Cigarette Dispenser Catalin Plastic, 4$^{1/4}$" x 5$^{3/4}$"
Closed   Open

Dunhill Lighter and Cigarette Dispenser, 8$^{1/4}$" x 3$^{1/2}$"
Open   Closed

Wooden Donkey Cigarette Dispenser, 8$^{1/2}$" x 10$^{1/2}$" x 3$^{1/2}$"

Wooden Cigarette Dispenser
(Push bird down to get cigarette) 3$^{1/2}$" x 6$^{3/4}$"

Wood Cigarette Dispenser 3$^{3/4}$" x 4" x 3"

Closed   Open

Cigarette Dispenser, Cigarette in Mouth, 6¹/²" x 7¹/²"

When Button on Right is Depressed Cigarette Appears as Photo at Left

Copper Cigar Holder Made to Look Like a Wine Bottle, 9" x 2¹/²" (Open)

Cigar Holder (Closed)

Cigarette Cases

Very Early Auto Ashtray, Match
Holder, Cigarette Holder Combo;
Circa 1920; 3$^{1/4}$" x 3" x 3$^{1/4}$"

Top: Brass Cigarette Case, 4$^{3/4}$" x 3$^{3/8}$" x $^{1/2}$"
Bottom: Brass Cigarette Case, 5$^{1/2}$" x 3$^{1/4}$" x $^{3/8}$"

Cigarette Case and Liquor Flask Made in Germany,
4$^{1/4}$" x 4" x $^{3/4}$"

Closed

Assortment of Cigarette Cases
Top Left-4" x 2¼" x ½", Nazi, Made in Germany; Top Right- 3½" x 2⅛" x ¾", Metal with Magic Compartments, 3½" x 2⅛" x ¾"; Middle Left- 3⅝" x 2⅜" x 1⅛", Princess Gardner, ; Middle Right- Tin Case, 3" x 2⅛" x 1"; Bottom- 3¾" x 3⅛" x 5/16" Brass with Polar Bear Scene, 3¾" x 3⅛"

Top Left- Plastic Cigarette Case, Bavaria 1945 2" x 3"; Top Right- Plastic Cigarette Case 2" x 3"; Bottom- Plastic Cigarette Case 2¼" x 3"

Rhinestone   Cigarette Case USA
3½" x 2¼" x 1⅛"

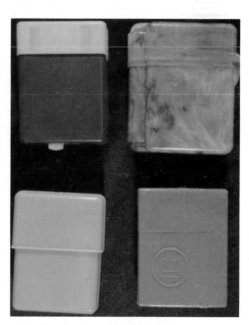

op Left- 3" x 4", Top Right- 2¼" x 3½"; ottom Left- 2" x 23/4" Push into Pack; Bottom Right- Cigarette Box 2½" x 3"

Top Left- Plastic Cigarette Case "Roger Slide" Made by Rogers Imports, Inc. Top Right- Cigarette Case with Lighter Bottom Left- Plastic Cigarette Case Made By Beacon; Bottom Right- Plastic Cigarette Case Made By Plas-Tex

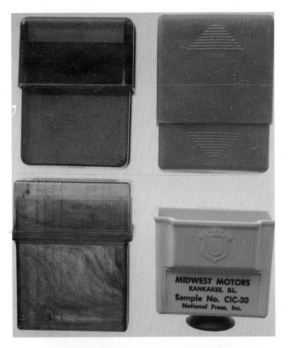

Cigarette
Cases
All 3 x 2¹ᐟ⁴"
Except
Bottom Right
2" x 2¹ᐟ²"

#1, 3" x 3⁷ᐟ⁸"; #2, 3" x 4"; #3, 3¹ᐟ⁴" x 3⁵ᐟ⁸";
#4, 4³ᐟ⁴" x 3¹ᐟ²"

Leather Fatima Cigarette Pack Holder Gold Foil
Stamped on Back "Annual Fumigation of Jesup
Hall Given under the Auspices of Senior Class
March 11, 1913"

Top Left- 2" x 2³ᐟ⁴"; Top Right- 2 x 3¹ᐟ⁴";
Bottom Right- Leather, 2¹ᐟ⁴" x 3¹ᐟ²";
Bottom Right- 3¹ᐟ⁴" x 2¹ᐟ²"

Cigarette Box - Match Box Metal Buttons-Plastic Italy,
Cigarette Box, 3⁵ᐟ⁸" x 1⁵ᐟ⁸" x 1",
Match Box Holder 1⁵ᐟ⁸" x 1¹ᐟ⁸" x ⁵ᐟ⁸"

Cigarette Lighters with Cases

Lighter and
Cigarette Box

Top-Art Deco Marathon
"Lady Lite" Lighter and
Cigarette Case
$2^{3/4}$" x $^{1/2}$" x $2^{3/4}$"

Bottom-Art Deco Marathon
Marking Lighter and
Cigarette Case
3" x $^{1/2}$" x $4^{1/2}$"

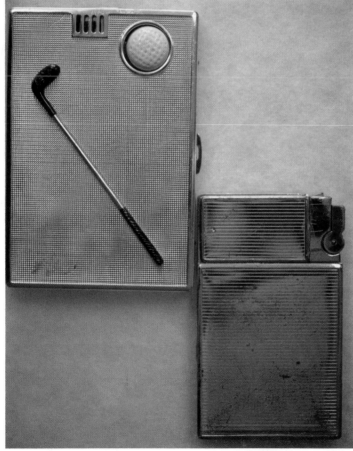

Top-"800 Eagle" Lighter and
Cigarette Case with Golfball
as the lighters trigger
3" x $^{1/2}$" x $4^{1/2}$"

Bottom-A.S.R. Lighter and
Cigarette Case,
$2^{1/4}$" x $^{1/2}$" x 4"

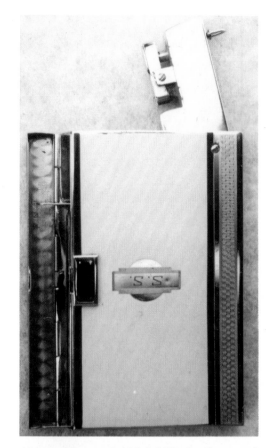

1930's Ronson Art Metal Works Case and
Lighter Combo, 4¹/²" x 3"

Lighter, Cigarette Case, and Compact Combos
Top Left-1930's Marathon, Pat. No. 1921855, 3³/⁴" x 2⁵/⁸"
Bottom Right-Evans, Pat No. 80179, 4³/⁸" x 2¹/⁴"

Ronson Compact, Case and Lighter Combos
Top-Black Enamel, 4¹/⁴"
Bottom-Floral Pattern with Tortoise Style Enamel,
3¹/⁴"

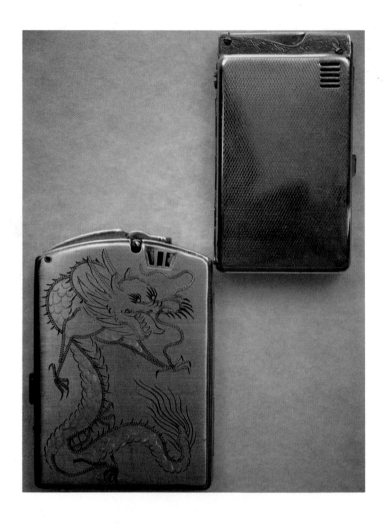

Top-"Atom" Terra Japan
Lighter and Cigarette Case,
Made in Occupied Japan,
2" x 1/2" x 3³/4"

Bottom-Victory Lighter and
Cigarette Case with Engraved
Dragon, 3" x 1/2" x 4"

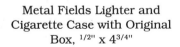

Metal Fields Lighter and
Cigarette Case with Original
Box, 1/2" x 4³/4"

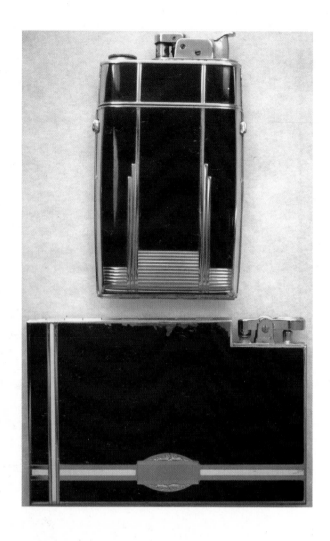

Top-Art Deco Evans Lighter
and Cigarette Case
2¹/₄" x ¹/₂" x 4¹/₄"

Bottom-Art Deco Ronson
Lighter and Cigarette Case
4³/₄" x ³/₈" x 3"

Plastic Cigarette Pack Holder
and Lighter
2³/₄" x 1" x 3¹/₄"

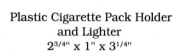

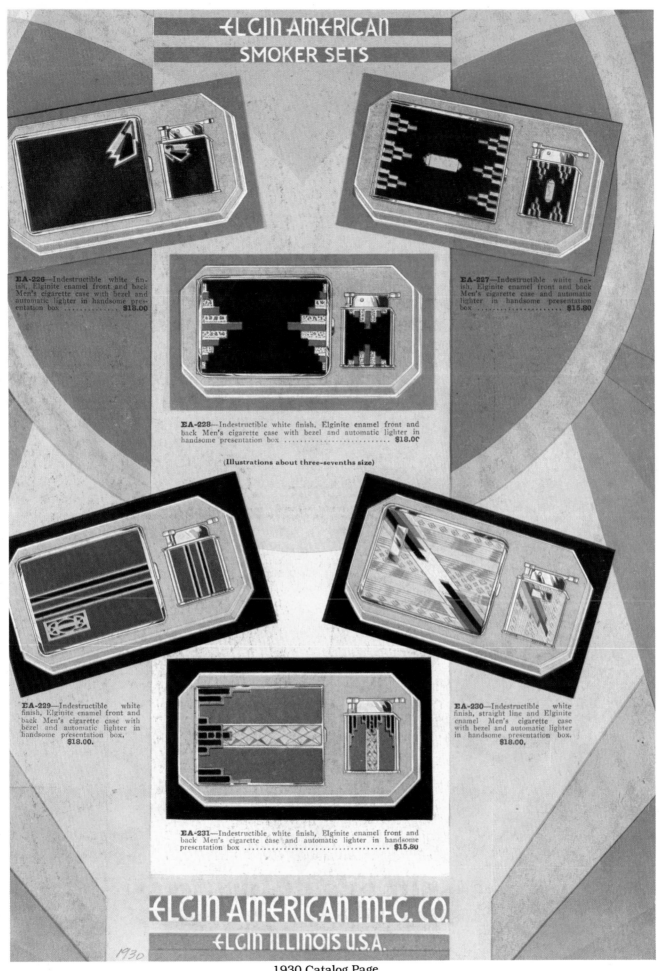

ELGIN AMERICAN
SMOKER SETS

EA-226—Indestructible white finish, Elginite enamel front and back Men's cigarette case with bezel and automatic lighter in handsome presentation box $18.00

EA-227—Indestructible white finish, Elginite enamel front and back Men's cigarette case and automatic lighter in handsome presentation box $15.80

EA-228—Indestructible white finish, Elginite enamel front and back Men's cigarette case with bezel and automatic lighter in handsome presentation box $18.00

(Illustrations about three-sevenths size)

EA-229—Indestructible white finish, Elginite enamel front and back Men's cigarette case with bezel and automatic lighter in handsome presentation box. $18.00.

EA-230—Indestructible white finish, straight line and Elginite enamel Men's cigarette case with bezel and automatic lighter in handsome presentation box. $18.00.

EA-231—Indestructible white finish, Elginite enamel front and back Men's cigarette case and automatic lighter in handsome presentation box $15.80

ELGIN AMERICAN MFG. CO.
ELGIN ILLINOIS U.S.A.

1930

1930 Catalog Page

113

N970—Gold lined men's cigarette case in hammered engine turned design with automatic Roller Bearing pocket lighter to match in attractive Gift Box......$9.00 ea.

N971—Genuine leather cigarette case to hold twenty cigarettes, lizard grain with automatic Roller Bearing pocket lighter to match in attractive Gift Box....$9.00 ea.

N972—Gold lined men's cigarette case in genuine hand engine turned and brocade design with automatic Roller Bearing pocket lighter to match in attractive Gift Box.........................$12.00 ea.

N973—Gold lined men's cigarette case in striking modernistic design in assorted colors of French enamel with automatic Roller Bearing pocket lighter to match in attractive Gift Box...........$13.50 ea.

N974—Double bezel cigarette case French enamel back and front in assorted contrasting colors, with automatic Roller Bearing pocket lighter to match in attractive Gift Box................$15.00 ea.

N975—Thin model gold lined men's cigarette case in contrasting colors of French enamel with egg shell effect with automatic Roller Bearing pocket lighter to match in attractive Gift Box.................$22.50 ea.

N976—Green gold finish, double bezel cigarette case, genuine leather cover in black lizard design with shield and automatic Roller Bearing pocket lighter to match in attractive Gift Box.....$16.50 ea.

N977—Gold lined ladies' cigarette case, French enamel front in assorted colors with contrasting neutral initial monogram design and automatic Roller Bearing pocket lighter to match in attractive Gift Box. $14.50 ea.

N978—Genuine ostrich cigarette case to hold twenty cigarettes with automatic Roller Bearing pocket lighter to match in attractive Gift Box............$14.25 ea.

Illustrations two-third size.

The LINE with the STERLING TOUCH

1930 Catalog Page

114

EC313—Gold lined Men's Cigarette Case in hammered design with Automatic Roller Bearing Pocket Lighter to match in attractive gift box.............$6.00 ea.

EC314—Gold lined Ladies' Cigarette Case, brocade and engine turned design with Automatic Roller Bearing Pocket Lighter to match in attractive gift box.....$6.00 ea.

EC315—Gold lined Men's Cigarette Case, French enamel front with egg shell effect with Automatic Roller Bearing Pocket Lighter to match in attractive gift box. $15.00 ea.

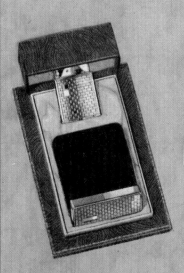

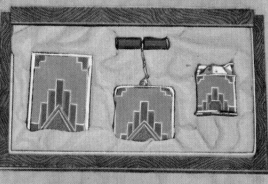

EC317—Gold lined Ladies' Cigarette Case, modernistic design in French enamel front with double compact, lipstick handle and Automatic Roller Bearing Pocket Lighter to match in attractive gift box.................................$16.50 ea.

EC316—Automatic Servpac Cigarette Case to hold 20 package of cigarettes with genuine leather body in Hudson grain, with Automatic Roller Bearing Pocket Lighter to match, in attractive gift box. $9.75 ea.

EC318—Automatic Servpac Cigarette Case to hold 20 package of cigarettes, modernistic design French enamel top with egg shell effect, genuine leather body in red Morocco grain with Automatic Roller Bearing Pocket Lighter to match in attractive gift box.....$14.25 ea.

EC319—Thin, knife edge model, gold lined Men's Cigarette Case, French enamel front with genuine Cloisonne enamel decoration with Automatic Roller Bearing Pocket Lighter to match in attractive gift box.............$18.00 ea.

EC320—Automatic Servpac Cigarette Case to hold 20 package of cigarettes, French enamel top with genuine Cloisonne enamel decoration, genuine ostrich body with Automatic Roller Bearing Pocket Lighter to match in attractive gift box. ....$15.00 ea.

EC321—Gold lined thin model Ladies' Cigarette Case, all over French enamel front and back with genuine Marcassite decoration, Automatic Roller Bearing Pocket Lighter to match in attractive gift box. ....$18.00 ea.

ILLUSTRATIONS ONE-THIRD ACTUAL SIZE EXCEPT EC317, WHICH IS ONE-HALF ACTUAL SIZE

World's Largest Manufacturers of Style Accessories

Cigarette and Cigar Holders

Display Card of Three Cigarette Holders
$3^{3/4}$" x $4^{7/8}$"

Display Card of Three Cigarette Holders
$3^{1/4}$" x $4^{7/8}$"

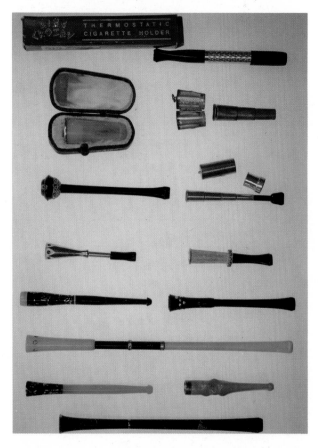

#1, 4"; #4, $3^{7/8}$"; #5, 3"; #6, $2^{3/4}$"; #7, $2^{1/2}$"; #8, $3^{7/8}$";
#9, $3^{7/8}$"; #10, 8"; #11, $3^{3/4}$"; #12, $2^{3/4}$"; #13, $6^{1/8}$"

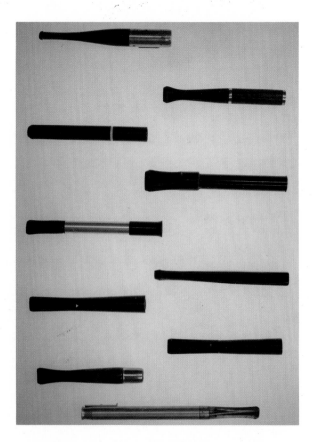

#1, $3^{15/16}$"; #2, $3^{1/2}$"; #4, $4^{3/16}$"; #5, $4^{1/8}$"; #6, 4";
#7, $3^{1/2}$"; #8, $3^{3/8}$"; #9, $3^{1/4}$"; #10, $5^{5/16}$"

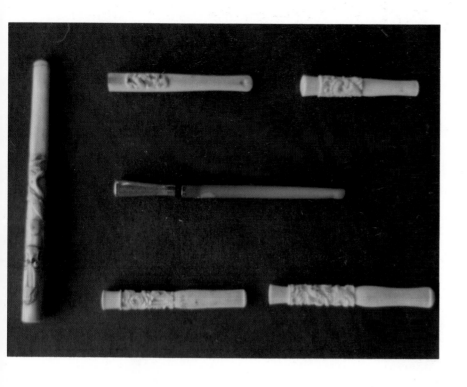

Cigarette Holders, All Ivory Except Middle
Top Left 3$^{1/2}$" Long
Top Right 2$^{3/4}$" Long
Middle-Plastic Amber and Metal,
5$^{1/4}$" Long
Bottom Left 3$^{1/2}$" Long
Bottom Right 4" Long
Left 6" Long

Top Left-Cigarette Holders both 3" Long
Bottom Left-Bullholder with Case, 3$^{3/4}$" Long
Top-Cigar Holder Bakelite, 2$^{3/4}$" Long
Top Middle-Cigar Holder, 2$^{1/2}$" Long
Bottom Middle-Cigar Holder, 2$^{3/4}$" Long
Bottom-Bakelite Cigar Holder, 2$^{1/2}$" Long

Display Card of Cigarette Holders
10³/₄" x 6"

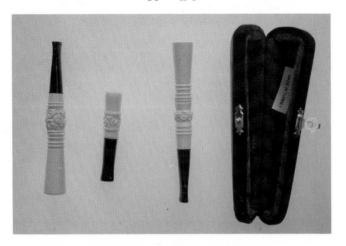

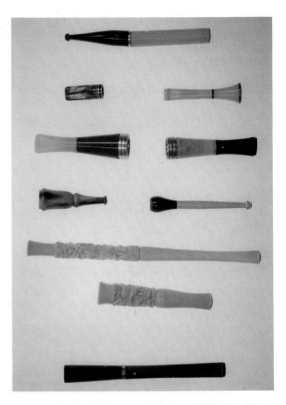

#1, 4³/₈"; #2, 1¹/₈"; #3, 2⁵/₁₆"; #4, 2¹³/₁₆"; #5, 2³/₄";
#6, 2"; #7, 3¹/₁₆"; #8, 7"; #9, 3¹/₂"; #10, 4¹³/₁₆"

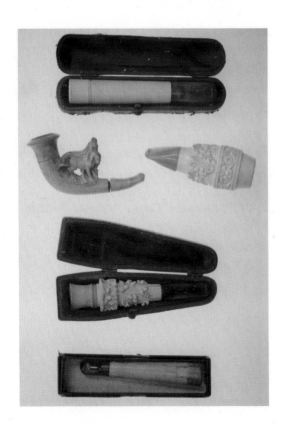

#1, 4"; #2, 3¹/₄"; #3, 3"; #4, 3³/₄"; #5, 3¹/₄"

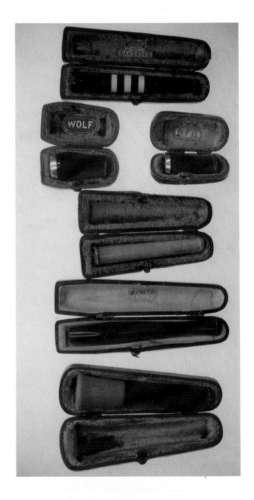

#1, 3³/₈"; #2, 1⁵/₈"; #3, 1¹/₂"; #4, 3";
#5, 4"; #6, 3⁵/₈"

118

Cigarette Boxes

Cigarette and Match Box Set Nickel Plated Occupied Japan
10" x 5$^{1/4}$"

Cigarette Holder with Four Hanging Ashtrays, Marked
Hand Painted TWNO Made in Japan,
4" x 5" x 5"

Wood Cigarette Holder with Two Ashtrays
and Calendar, 8$^{1/4}$" x 4$^{3/4}$" x6$^{5/8}$"

Wooden Cigarette Holder Opened Up

Soapstone Cigarette Dispenser
4¹/₈" x 1³/₄" x 2¹/₂"

Composition Ashtray Cigarette Box, USA,
10³/₄" x 5¹/₂" x 1³/₄"

Girlie Art Deco Cigarette
Pack Holder and Dispenser
4³/₄" x ¹/₂" x 3"

Cigarette Box with Gold Trim,
4" x 2¹/₂" x 2¹/₂"

Souvenir Pipe Rest, Cigarette Box, Ashtray
10¹/₂" x 6" x 2"

Cigarette Box and Ashtray
7 x 4 x 1$^{1/2}$"

Nickel Silver Electro Plated Silver USA Cigarette Box
4$^{1/2}$" x 3$^{1/4}$" x 1$^{1/2}$"

Store Cigarette Sampler, Chrome, Circa 1930
10$^{1/2}$" x 1" x 3$^{3/4}$"

Ronson Touch Tip and Cigarette Box, 8¹/₂"

Striker and Cigarette Pack Holder, Brass, Germany, 4" x 7"

Ronson Monkey Pick-A-Cig Striker, Enameled Box, Deco, 1930's, 5" x 8³/₈"

Ronson Touch Tip and Cigarette Holder, Rolltop Chrome and Enamel, 7¹/₄" x 6"

Art Deco Ashtrays

Smoking Set Match Holder also comes with:
Cigarette Box 7⁷/₈" x 3¹/₂" x 2", Ashtray 3³/₈" x 2³/₄" x ³/₄"

Art Deco Bull Dog Ashtray by Hamilton
5³/₄" x 3¹/₄"

Art Deco Bull Dog Ashtray by Central Die
Casting and Mfg. Co. 4¹/₄" x 7"

Art Deco Squirrel Ashtray with
Cigarette Holder and Snuffer in the
Middle, By Hamilton, 2³/₄" x 5³/₄"

Art Deco Women's Head Ashtray, Head is a
Smoky-Frosted Glass, 6³/₄" x 4"

Art Deco Cast Aluminum Ashtray
with Venice Boat, $4^{3/8}$" x $3^{3/8}$" x $2^{3/4}$"

Art Deco Ashtray with Figural Horse,
7" x $4^{3/4}$" x $6^{1/4}$"

Farber Brothers Art Deco Ashtray,
USA, $6^{3/4}$" x $4^{3/4}$" x $1^{3/4}$"

Art Deco Figural Ashtray with
Match Holder, Daka-Ware, Chicago,
5" x 6"

Art Deco Ball Ashtray,
$3^{1/4}$" x 2"

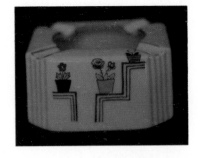

Art Deco Toilet Seat Ashtray,
Made in England, 4" x $2^{1/4}$"

Art Deco Hand Painted
Ashtray, Trico Nagoya-Japan,
$1^{3/4}$" x $3^{3/4}$" x $3^{3/4}$"

Art Deco Ashtray with Snuffers in the
Middle, Snuffer is Bakelite, 6" x $3^{1/4}$"

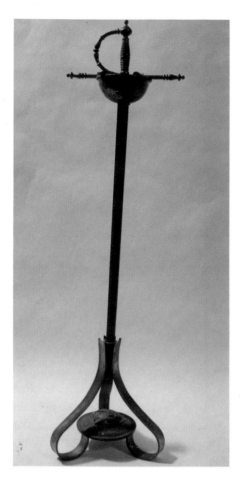

Sword Floor Ashtray 34¹/₂" x 9¹/₂"

Smoking Stand with Akro Agate Lighter,
Two Ashtrays and a Cigarette Holder
27¹/₂" x 10"

Art Deco Floor Ashtray Maker Unknown,
23" x 10¹/₂"

Art Deco Chrome Ashtray, USA, 5$^{1/2}$" x 2$^{1/2}$"

Elephant Art Deco Ashtray by Hamilton,
4$^{1/2}$" x 1$^{3/4}$"

Alligator Art Deco Ashtray
"Pincherette", 4$^{3/8}$" x 1$^{3/4}$"

Art Deco Cat Chrome Ashtray,
7$^{1/4}$" x 4$^{1/2}$" x 2$^{1/2}$"

Dog Art Deco Ashtray "Pincherette",
1$^{3/4}$" x 4$^{3/8}$"

Art Deco Chrome Ashtray, USA

Art Deco Hippo Ashtray "Pincherette",
1$^{3/4}$" x 4$^{3/8}$" x 1$^{3/4}$"

Cast Iron Ashtrays

Cast Iron Ashtray – USA. Base is Wilton Prod. #4.
(You can find these with many different bases, different
people and different signs. The men or women next to
the post's were originally bottle openers. 4³/₄" x 3³/₄",

Cast Iron Man on Post, Japan 4" x 4³/₄"

Cast Iron Ashtray with Comic
Advertising Tile,
Japan, 5" x 5" x 1"

Cast Iron Ashtray, 4³/₄" x 4"

Japan Ashtrays

Assorted Match Holders with Ashtrays
(All Made in Japan)

Left: Japan Asthray and Match Holder, 4¹/⁴" x 3³/⁴"
Right: Japan Ashtray, 3³/⁴" x 3¹/⁴" x 2¹/²"

Japan Ashtray, Cigarette Holder and
Match Holder with Three Black Children
3¹/²" x 4⁵/⁸" x 2⁷/⁸"

Black Child Ashtray
(Japan), 4" x 3¹/⁴" x 1¹/²"

Japan Ashtray and
Match Holder,
3¹/²" x 3¹/⁴" x 2¹/⁴"

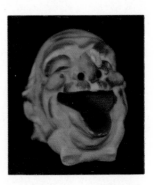

Man Ashtray with Bee
on Nose, Hand Painted,
3" x 4¹/²" x 3"

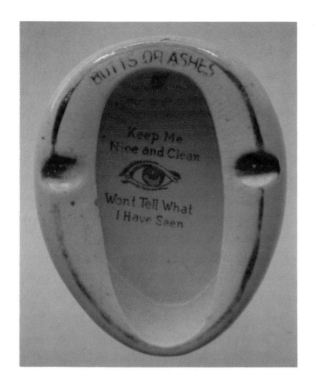

Japan Ashtray, 4¼" x 3½"

Top: Made in Japan, 3½" x 4½",
Bottom: Made in Japan 3" x 5"

Japan Ashtray, 4¼" x 3"

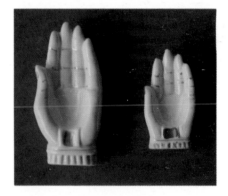

Japan Ashtrays, Left: 2" x 4"
Right: 2¾" x 1½"

Made in Occupied Japan, 3½" x 3¾"

Japan Ashtray, 4¼" x 3½" x 3"

Made in Japan Ashtrays, Left: 2$^{7/8}$" x 4" x 3$^{3/4}$"
Right: 3" x 4" x 2$^{7/8}$"

Assorted Novelty Ashtray and Cigarette Holders, Made in Japan,
All About 2$^{1/4}$"

Set of Japan Ashtrays, 3$^{1/2}$" x 2" x 2$^{3/4}$" x 2$^{7/8}$"

Ashtray and Ashtray Holder,
3" x 5" x 2$^{1/4}$"

Set of Four Japan Ashtrays,
4$^{1/2}$" x 1$^{7/8}$" x 1$^{1/2}$"

Left: Occupied Japan Novelty Match Holder,
Cigarette Holder, and Ashtray, 2$^{1/4}$" x 3$^{1/2}$" x 3"
Right: Japan Novelty Ashtray by H.F. and Co., 4" x 1$^{3/4}$"

Left: Japan Ashtray, 4" x 2$^{3/8}$"
Right: Occupied Japan Ashtray, 3$^{7/8}$" x 2$^{5/8}$" x 2$^{3/4}$"

Carved Wood Ashtray with Match Box Holder
on Back of Gnome, 5$^{1/2}$" x 6$^{1/4}$"

Black Porter Statue with Cigarette Pack Holder, Match Cover
Holder and Ashtray

Rubber Tire Ashtrays

Good Year Ashtray,
3^{1/2}" x 3^{1/2}"

Century of Progress,
5^{1/2}"

Dunlop Tire Advertising Ashtray,
6" x 1^{3/4}"

Seiberling Tires,
5^{1/2}" x 5^{1/2}"

The Advantage Ashtray,
5$^{1/2}$" x 5$^{1/2}$"

Good Year Ashtray,
5$^{1/2}$" x 5$^{1/2}$"

General Tire Ashtray,
6$^{1/2}$" x 6$^{1/2}$"

Tire Ashtray,
6" x 2"

Cigarette Lighters with Boxes

Deco, Ronson Touch-Tip Lighter with Cigarette Box Tray, 4³/⁴" x 12¹/⁴" x 4"

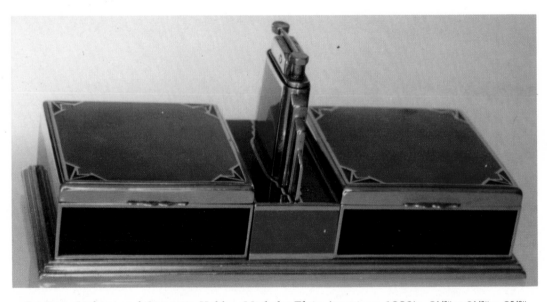

Art Deco Lighter and Cigarette Holder, Made by Elgin American 1930's, 3¹/²" x 8¹/²" x 3⁵/⁸"

Cigarette Lighter and Ashtray Sets

Akro Agate Ashtray and Lighter Set,
Base 5³/⁴" x 4" x ³/⁴"

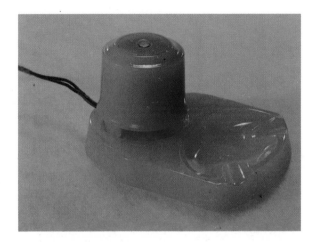

Akro Agate Glass Ashtray and Lighter Set
5" x 4" x 3³/⁴"

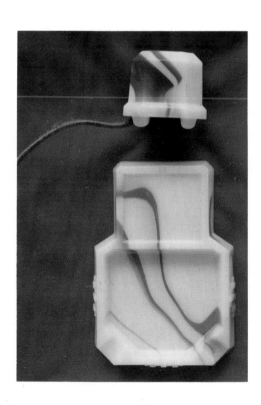

Akro Agate Ashtray and Electric Lighter
Combo

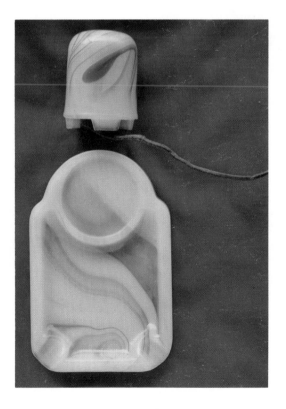

Akro Agate Ashtray and Electric Lighter
Combo

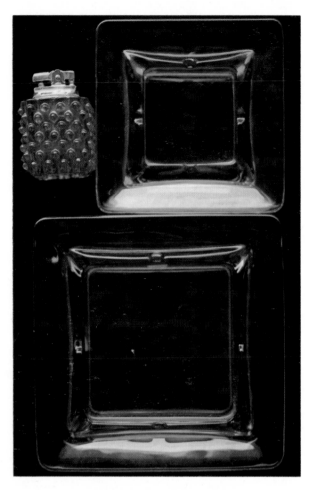

Glass Ashtrays and Lighter

Lighter Mug Set,
Lighter, 4" x 2^{1/2}" x 3^{1/4}"
Mug, 3^{3/4}" x 4^{3/4}"

Advertising Set Made by Brown and Bigelow,
Eight Ball Lighter and Bakelight Base,
7^{1/4}" x 5^{3/4}" x 3^{1/4}"

Marble Ashtray
and Lighter

Smoking Set
Cigarette Case, 4" x 3" x ^{1/2}";
Lighter, 1^{11/16}" x ^{1/2}" x 1^{1/4}";
Pill Box, 1^{3/4}" x 1^{1/2}" x ^{3/4}"
Lighter was made by Lester (Japan)

Evans Lighter and Ashtrays

Lighter, Ashtray and Cigarette Box Set

Lighter, Cigarette Holder, and Ashtray;
Fostoria Glass; Lighter 3" x 3³/₄";
Cigarette Holder 2¹/₂" x 2¹/₂"; Ashtray 5" x 2"

Lighter and Ashtray Set
Lighter 3¹/₂" x 3" x 2"
Ashtray 3¹/₄" x 3¹/₂" x 2¹/₄"

Sterling Silver Lighter and Ashtray

Lighter and Cigarette
Holder Set, Made in Japan,
Lighter 4$^{1/2}$" x 2$^{1/2}$",
Match Holder 3$^{1/2}$" x 2$^{1/2}$"

Crystal Set Made in Japan,
Lighter 2$^{1/4}$" x 3$^{3/4}$",
Ashtray 4$^{1/4}$" x 1$^{1/2}$"

Lighter and Ashtray Made in Japan

Evans Metal Set
Lighter 2" x 2$^{1/2}$"
Holder 2" x 1$^{1/2}$"

Occupied Japan Lighter, Cigarette Tray, and Cup

Cigarette Lighter, Tray and Dispenser;
Made in Korea

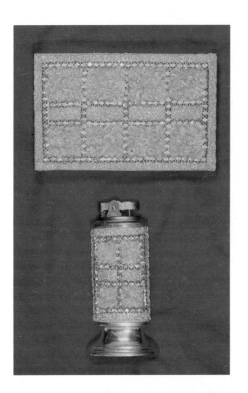

Evans Table Lighter and Cigarette
Box with Rhinestones

Made in Occupied Japan Smoking Set
Cigarette Holder 3 x 2$^{1/4}$"
Lighter 3$^{1/4}$" x 2$^{3/4}$"
Tray 6$^{1/4}$" x 4$^{1/4}$"

Ronson Art Pottery ashtray and lighter set.
Ashtray 3$^{3/4}$" x 6$^{1/2}$" x 5$^{1/2}$"
Lighter 3" x 3"

Lighter and Ashtray

Cigarette Dispenser, Ashtray, and
Lighter; German

Lighter and Cigarette Cup

Painted Cast Aluminum Ashtray and Lighter
6" x 5$^{1/2}$" x 4"

Cherub Lighter and Cigarette Cup,
Japan

140

Slag Lighter and Ashtray

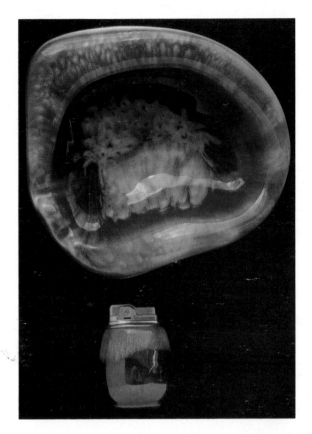

Royal Haeger Ashtray and Ronson Lighter

Japan Lighter and Ashtray

Tray and Lighter Combo

Pot Metal Bronze Plated Japan,
9$^{1/2}$" x 5"

Saschab Ashtray and Lighter,
Metal with Refinished
Ashtray 5$^{1/4}$", Lighter 4$^{1/4}$"

Evans Lighter and Tray, Italy,
Ashtray 8$^{1/2}$" x 1"
Lighter 2$^{1/2}$" x 5$^{3/4}$"

Smoking Set-Lighter, Ashtray and Cigarette Holder.
Cigarette Holder has Spring Loaded Bottom to Push
Cigarettes Up. Cigarette Holder-3$^{1/2}$" x 3$^{1/2}$",
Ashtray-4$^{1/2}$" x 4$^{1/2}$", Lighter-2" x 3"

Enameled Baggage Cart Lighter, Ashtray and
Cigarette Holder, Rubber Wheels, 3³/⁴" x 4¹/²"

1925 Lighter and Ashtray Set, Aimaiaikah, Los Angeles
Possibly Some Type of Lodge Symbol

Evans Lighters and Ashtray, Original Sticker Price in
Bronze Color $15.95, 9"

Lighter, Cigarette Holder and Ashtray, Brass,
Austria,, 4¹/²" x 5³/⁴"

Trench Art Lighters & Ashtrays

Trench Art Ashtray and Lighter, Lighter is in Center Bullet. 105mm Base 1944, 4$^{11/16}$" x 5$^{3/4}$"

World War II, Hand Made, 105mm Base Shell, 5" x 4$^{3/4}$"

Trench Art Lighter and Ashtray, Lighter 2" x 7", Ashtray 2$^{1/2}$" x 2"

Trench Art Ashtray and Lighter, Made in 1945 Shell Base was from 1905, 8" x 9"

Match Holder, 2$^{1/4}$" x 1$^{1/2}$" x $^{3/4}$"

Ashtrays with Built-in Lighters

Copper Ronson Striker Bulldog Lighter and Ashtray,
5" x 3$^{1/4}$" x 4"

Cast Aluminum Ashtray with Lighter in
Dog's Head, 5$^{7/8}$" x 5$^{1/4}$" x 4"

Dog Lighter with Head Taken Off

Strik-a-lite Ashtray and Lighter,
5" x 3$^{1/2}$" x 3"

Copper Advertising Ashtray and Lighter,
Potter Coal Co. Indianapolis, IN

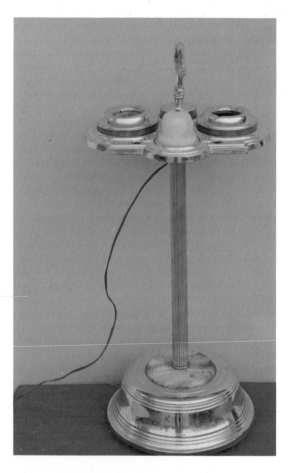

Circa 1950's Smoking Stand with Electric
Lighter, 27$^{1/2}$" x 10$^{1/2}$"

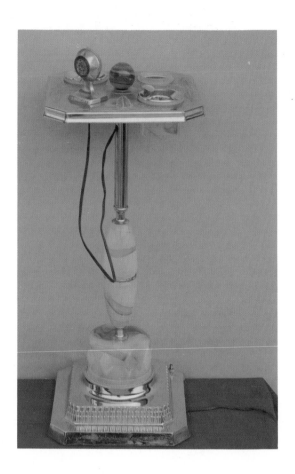

Circa 1950's Smoking Stand with Electric
Lighter, 27$^{1/2}$" x 10$^{1/2}$" x 10$^{1/2}$"

Occupied Japan Ashtray with Lighter in Plane,
5$^{1/2}$" x 6$^{1/2}$" x 8"

Miscellaneous Ashtrays

Brass Ashtray, Made in China,
$8^{3/4}$" x $6^{1/8}$" x 2"

Milk Glass Ashtray, $2^{1/4}$" x $4^{1/2}$" x $2^{1/4}$"

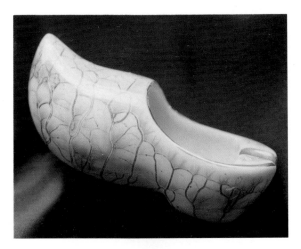

Ashtray Made in Holland, $4^{1/2}$" x 2" x 2"

Shoe Ashtrays, Made in India,
Top: $1^{1/4}$" x 4", Bottom: 2" x 7"

Novelty Ashtray – 5" x $4^{1/4}$"
(When you put your cigarette down
it triggers the boy to pee on the cigarette extinguishing it.)

Porcelain Ashtray, 5$^{1/2}$" x 6" x $^{3/4}$"

Set of Majolica Ashtrays
Top Ashtray-3$^{1/2}$" x 3$^{1/2}$" x 1"
Bottom Ashtray-4$^{1/2}$" x 4$^{1/2}$" x 1$^{1/4}$"
Top-#3735II, Bottom-#3900

German Ashtray, 3$^{3/4}$" x 3$^{3/4}$"

The Valencia Ashtray was Created at Craftacres Company
"was made to sit on armrest of a couch or chair.", 5$^{1/2}$" x 3"

Pocket Ashtrays,
Top-Brass Pocket Ashtray, 2$^{1/2}$" x 1$^{1/2}$" x $^{1/2}$",
Bottom-Art Deco Pocket Ashtray 2$^{1/2}$" x $^{3/4}$"

Pocket Ashtrays Open

Small Pocket Ashtray, 1$^{1/2}$" x $^{1/2}$"

Garbage Can Ashtray, Japan, 2" x 2$^{1/4}$"

Advertising
Pocket Ashtray,
2$^{1/4}$" x 1$^{1/2}$" x $^{3/4}$"

Advertising Pocket Ashtray with Original Box,
2$^{1/4}$" x 1$^{1/2}$" x $^{3/4}$"

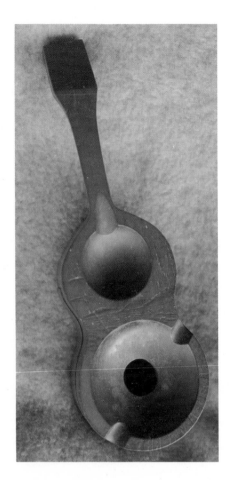 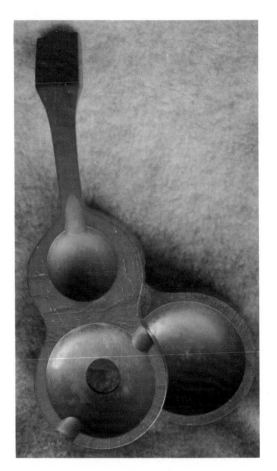

Wood Ashtray, 8$^{1/4}$" x 2$^{3/4}$" x 1$^{1/2}$"

Akro Agate Black Amethyst – 3" x 1"

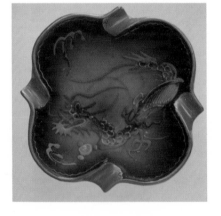

Japan Ashtray with Dragon Design. (This ashtray was part of a set of many items with this design. There is also other shapes and sizes of this ashtray.) 1" x 4$^{3/8}$" x 4$^{3/8}$"

Art Glass Ashtray Made in Italy, 2$^{3/4}$" x 1$^{1/4}$"

Glass and Metal Ashtray with Etching in Glass, 2$^{5/8}$" x 2$^{5/8}$" x 3^{4}"

Naughty Ashtray (Front), 4¹/₂" x 5³/₄"   Back

Fostoria Ashtray, 1" x 3³/₄" x 3¹/₈"

Ashtray and Cigarette Holder, Cast Iron
and Wood, 5" x 6¹/₄" x 6¹/₂"

151

Akro Agate Ashtray With Figural Dog, 5$^{1/2}$" x 4$^{1/8}$"

Akro Agate Ashtray with Figural Lion,
7$^{3/4}$" x 4$^{1/2}$" x 3$^{1/4}$"

Metal Ashtray, 3$^{3/4}$" x 5" x 1$^{3/4}$"

Chase USA Ashtray 4$^{1/4}$" x 5$^{3/4}$"

Black Amethyst Chase Brass Top
Early Chase Mark, 2" x 3$^{1/4}$" 3"

Souvenir Ashtray, Circa 1930, 5$^{3/4}$" x 1$^{1/2}$"

Wedgwood Queensware, 5³/⁴"

Hall Ashtray, 4¹/⁴"

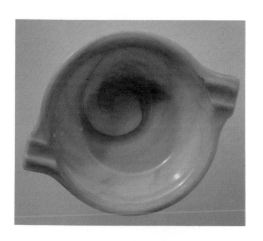

Akro Agate Ashtray, 3³/⁴"

Bottom to Above Hall Ashtray

Alacite Alladdin, 3¹/²" x 1¹/⁸"

Wedgwood Black Jasperware, 4¹/²"

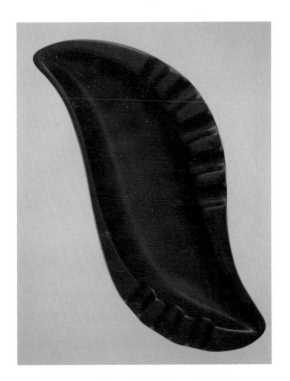

Black Roseville Ashtray Marked
Roseville USA, 7$^{1/2}$" x 3$^{1/4}$" x 1$^{1/4}$"

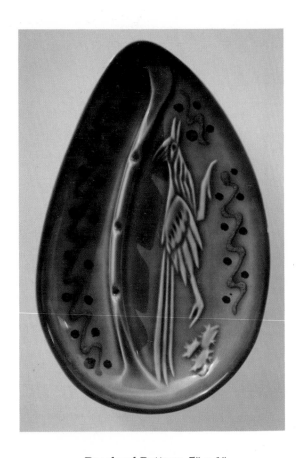

Roseland Pottery, 5" x 1"

Snuf-A-Rette Ashtray with
Advertising on Side, 1" x 3$^{5/8}$" x 2$^{3/4}$"

Stafford China Co. Ashtray Black Poodle,
Circa 1950's, 6" x 4$^{3/4}$" x 2$^{1/8}$"

Backside to Above Picture

Cast Bronze, USA, 3$^{1/4}$"

Metal Ashtray, Japan, 7$^{1/2}$"

Pottery Ashtray and Match Box Holder,
Masaic Tile Co., Zanesville, OH

Ashtray and Cigarette Holder Set.
Circa 1925, 4$^{1/4}$" x 4$^{1/4}$"

Copper Cowboy Hat Ashtray, 5$^{3/4}$" x 2"

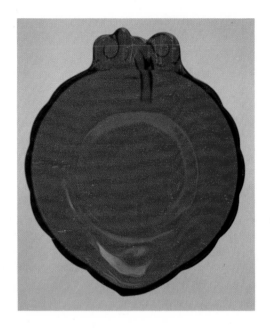

Ruby Glass Ashtray,
$5^{1/4}$" x $4^{3/8}$" x 1"

China Ashtray, Belleek Ireland,
1" x $4^{1/2}$"

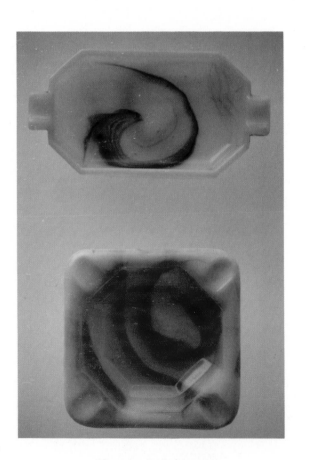

Akro Agate Ashtrays,
Bottom: 3" x 3" x $7/8$"
Top: $7/8$" x $2^{1/8}$" x $4^{1/8}$"

St. Clair Ashtray, Made in Elwood, IN
2" x $5^{1/2}$" x $4^{3/8}$"

Brass USA, 7" x 4$^{1/2}$"

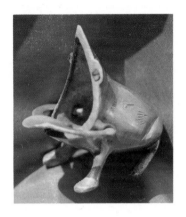

Frog Ashtray,
2$^{1/2}$" x 1$^{3/4}$" x 2$^{1/2}$"

Alligator Ashtray, Japan,
7" x 3" x 3$^{1/4}$"

Frog Ashtray 1934
Century of Progress,
5$^{1/2}$" x 2"

Pottery Elephant
Ashtray Holder and Three Ashtrays,
Made in Occupied Japan,
6" x 3" x 3"

Green Opaque Glass Ashtray with
Match Holder, 4³/₈" x 4³/₈" x 1"

Green Depression Glass
Ashtray with Flower
Design, 4¹/₂" x 3" x ³/₄"

Green Depression Glass Ashtray with
Match Holder, 3" x 4³/₄" x 4³/₄"

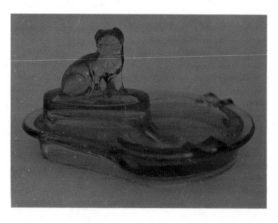

Peach Depression Glass Ashtray with Figural
Cat, 2⁷/₈" x 5³/₈" x 4¹/₂"

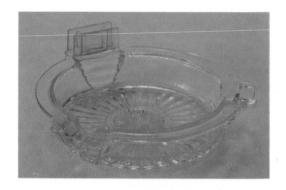

Depression Green Glass Ashtray with
Match Holder, 5¹/₈" x 1⁵/₈"

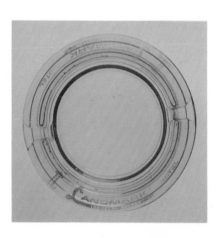

Green Glass Ashtray Advertising
Landmark Hotel, Las Vegas
Nevada, 4" x 1"

Green Depression Glass Ashtray,
4" x ³/₄"

Depression Green Glass
Ashtray, 4⁵/₈" x 4⁵/₈" 1¹/₄"

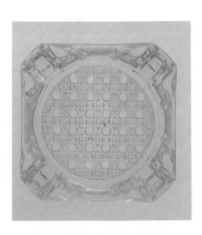

Green Depression Glass
Ashtray, ³/₄" x 3¹/₄" x 3¹/₄"

Japan, 5$^{1/2}$" x 4" x 3$^{1/2}$"

Pipe Ashtray, 6" x 2$^{3/4}$" x 3"

Cast Copper Masonic Ashtray, 4$^{5/16}$" x 4$^{5/16}$" x $^{5/8}$"

Cast Aluminum Ashtray No. 16 O.E.S.,
5$^{3/16}$" x $^{7/8}$"

Cast Aluminum Painted Masonic Ashtray,
5$^{1/2}$" x 1"

Set of Four Ashtrays Made in Occupied Japan,
2⁵/₈"

Set of McCoy Pottery Ashtrays Marked,
"McCoy USA", 4¹/₁₆"

Leather Covered Wood Cigarette Box Made in England with Niagara
Falls Advertising, 4¹/₂" x 3³/₈" x 2¹/₄"

Pipe Rest, Captain Black, 1¹/₄" x 3"

Special Ashtrays

Musical Knight Lighter and Smoking Set on Tray

Brass Lamp with Cigar Rests, Match Holder and
Cigar or Cigarette Holder, 7" x 7" x 8"

Roulette Wheel Ashtray Made in Japan. 5" x 5"

Metal Ship Wheel Ashtray made by Chase,
USA 6$^{1/4}$"

Limoges Ashtray Made in France, 4$^{1/2}$" x $^{7/8}$"

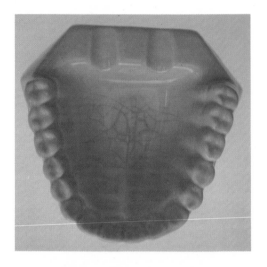

Mouth Shaped Dentist Ashtray,
4$^{1/4}$" x 4$^{1/2}$" x 1$^{1/2}$"

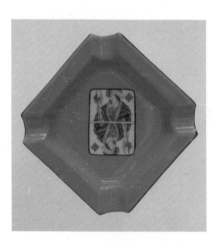

Porcelain Ashtray Made by Union
K in Czechoslovakia #183,
3$^{1/8}$" x 3$^{1/8}$" x $^{5/8}$"

Apple Ashtray with Metal Accessory (this metal
accessory was made to use on many different trays
to make an ashtray out of them.) 3" x 4$^{1/4}$" x 4$^{1/4}$"

Risque Aluminum Ashtray,
5¹/₄" x 3¹/₂" x ³/₄"

Back Side

Van Briggle Ashtray,
5¹/₄" x 3¹/₂" x ³/₄"

Back Side

Favorite Bavaria, 5" x 2"

Ashtray and Matchbox Holder Hand Painted Nippon
Ashtray 3$^{1/2}$" x 4"
Matchbox Holder 2$^{1/2}$" x 2"

Bavarian Ashtray
4$^{1/4}$" x 4$^{1/4}$"

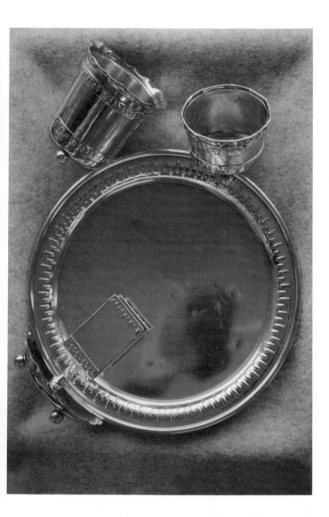

Copper Brass Smoking Set with Tray and
Match Box Holder, Tray, 9¹/₂", Ashtray 2³/₄" x 2¹/₄",
Match Holder 4" x 4", Cigarette Holder 3³/₈" x 3¹/₂"

Nippon Ashtray, 6³/₄" x 1¹/₄"

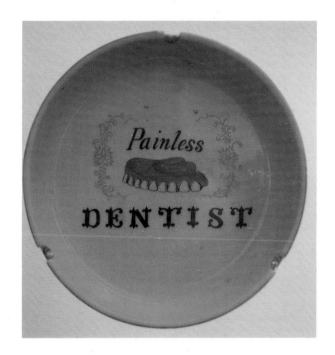

Dentist Ashtray with Gold Trim 5¹/₂" x 1¹/₂"

Nodder Ashtray, Made in USA, 5¹/₂" x 5"

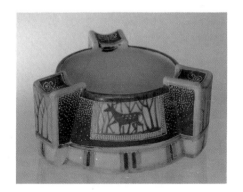

Nippon Ashtray 4³/₄" x 2¹/₄"

Advertising Ashtrays

Advertising Ashtray, 6" x 4"

Champion Sparkplug Ashtray,
$4^{1/2}$" x $4^{1/2}$"

Red Enamel Wagner Ware Ashtray #1050,
$4^{1/2}$" x 6"

Wagner Ware Cast Iron Ashtray #1050,
$4^{1/2}$" x 6"

Indy 500 Ashtray, Circa 1964, 7" x 7"

Advertising Ashtray, Circa 1915, 4$^{1/4}$" x 1$^{1/2}$"

Indianapolis Motor Speedway Ashtray,
Made in Japan, 5$^{1/2}$"

Cast Iron D.R. Plant Ashtray,
1970 Disamatic, 4$^{1/2}$" x 1"

Glass, 4$^{3/4}$" x 3" x 1$^{1/8}$"

Advertising Ashtray, 6¼"

Rookwood Pottery Ashtray advertising Boss Kerosene
Ranges, Stoves, Ovens and Heaters, Huenefeld Co.
1827-1947, Cincinnati Ohio USA – 5¾" x 1"

The Robinson
Clay Products
Co. Akron Ohio,
5⅜" x 1"

Glass Kool
Advertising
Ashtray, 5¼" x 1"

Planter Peanut Advertising Ashtray, USA,
5¾" x 4¾"

Mercedes Stefel Porcelain Ashtray, 3¾" x 4½"

China Ashtray, 5¹/⁴" x 5¹/⁴"

Advertising Ashtray, 7" x 4¹/²" x 4"

Advertisng Ashtray 4" x 3" x 2"

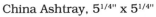

Porcelain Benson and Hedges
Advertising Ashtray, 4" x 1"

Standard Advertising Ashtray
Match Box Holder, 3¹/⁴" x 4³/⁴" x 4"

Heat Resistant Bakelite Ashtray,
Advertising Allison General Motors
4¹/²" x 4¹/²" x 1¹/¹⁶"

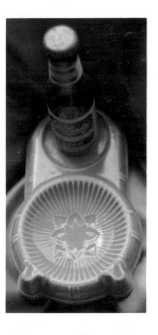

Advertising Blatz Beer
Ashtray, 5" x 3" x 4¹/⁴"

Miscellaneous

Black Nodder, Occupied Japan,
Pat. No. 95214, 4³/⁴"

Match Pull and Ashtray, Akro Agate Base,
Cincinnatti, OH Hamilton Match Co.
Pat. April 1935, 5¹/²" x 5¹/⁴"

Advertising Dunhill Pitcher, Made by Wade,
England, 7" x 3¹/⁴" x 6¹/²"

American Pull Match Piqua, OH,
US Pat. 2,014,182, 5¹/⁴" x 7"

Kool Cigarette Case

Cigarette Holder with Silver Case

Bracelet with Marlboro, Helmar, Raleigh, Kool,
Regent, Parliament, Herbert Tareytone, and
Camel Cigarette Charms

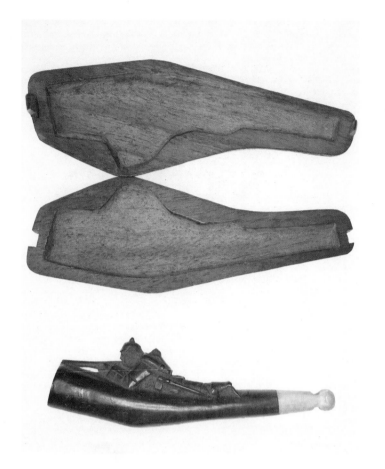

Hand Carved Cigarette Holder with Hand Carved Case,
Circa 1916, Made by French, Case 4" x 1$^{1/4}$",
Holder 3$^{1/2}$" x $^{1/2}$" x 1"

Raleigh Cigarette Counter Change Receiver,
7$^{1/2}$" x 7$^{1/2}$"

Cigar Case Sterling Silver, USA,
5$^{3/4}$" x 3$^{1/4}$"

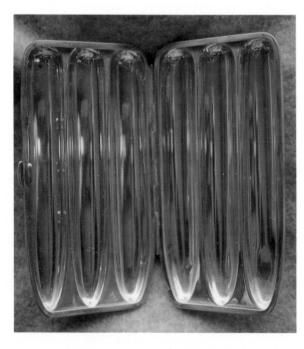

Opened Cigar Case

Cigarette Case and Lighter Smoking Set, Evans
Trig-A-Lite Lighter, Cigarette Case-2⁷/₈" x 3³/₄",
Lighter-1¹/₂" x 2"

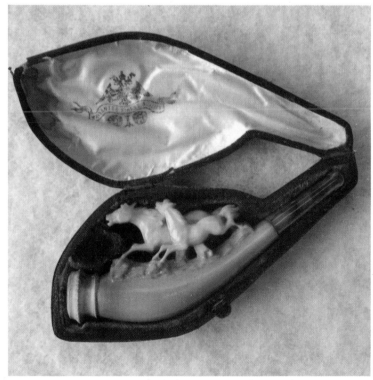

Meerschaum Cigar Holder in Leather Case, 4¹/₄" x 1³/₄"

Tin Cigarette Boxes

Tin Cigarette Boxes

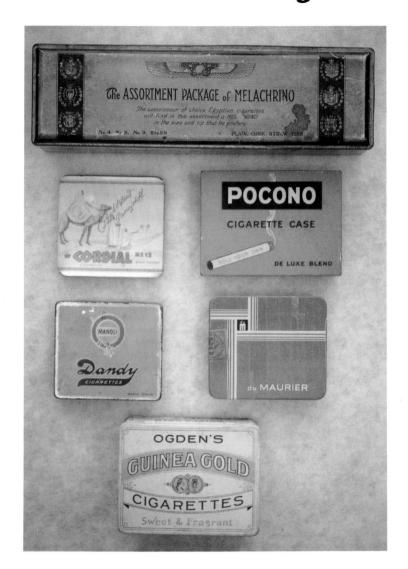

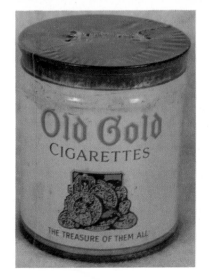

Hard Pack Cigarettes

*Note different printing on English Ovals

*Note different printing on Gitanes

Hard Pack Cigarettes

*Marlboro Pack is before Surgeon General Warning

Hard Pack Cigarettes

Inside view of Palette Cigarettes

*Note different printing on Rameses II

178

Hard Pack Cigarettes

Inside view of Sobranie Black and Gold Cigarettes

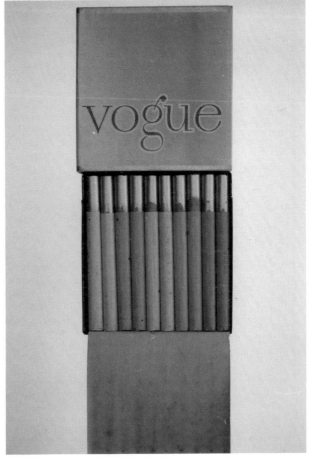

Inside view of Vogue Cigarettes

179

Soft Pack Cigarettes

Soft Pack Cigarettes

*Note 1st pack of Blue Cauloises has
Surgeon Generals Warning the second one does not.

Soft Pack Cigarettes

Soft Pack Cigarettes

*Note "Genuine Horse Shit Cigarettes"
has an Alas brand under it.

*Note "1st pack of Lion's has "King of Them All" on back

Soft Pack Cigarettes

*Note the two Marvel Cigarette Packs have
different printing on the back

Soft Pack Cigarettes

*Note first pack of Raleigh's has the coupon
second pack does not.

*Note first Rameses is Pre-WWII the second
Rameses is a later version

Soft Pack Cigarettes

*Note WIOU Cigarettes is a "Your Name Cigarettes"

*Note All above is "Your Name Cigarettes"

*Note top four is "Your Name Cigarettes"

Cardboard Cigarette Boxes

Gift Box with Assortment of the American Tobacco Co.

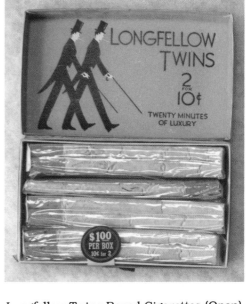

Longfellow Twins Boxed Cigarettes (Open)

Gift Box Opened

Hard Pack or Boxed Cigarettes

Hard Pack or Boxed Cigarettes

Cardboard Cigarette Boxes

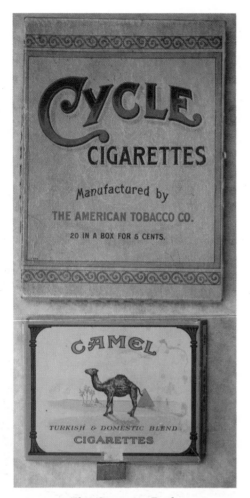

Inside View of Princess Cigarettes

Flat Cigarette Packs

Cigarette
Boxes

Sample Cigarettes

Political Cigarettes

Pipes

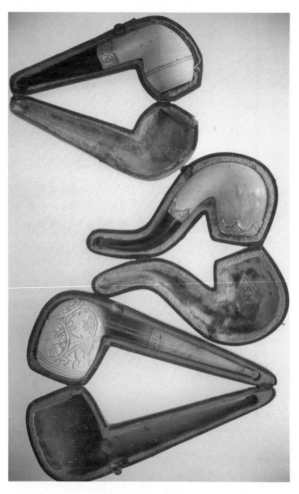

Top-Meerschaum Pipe with Case, 6¼" x 2",
Middle-Meerschaum Pipe with Gold Decorations
with Case, 5" x 2", Bottom-Meerschaum Pipe,
Amber Tip, Gold Decoration with Case, 5" x 2"

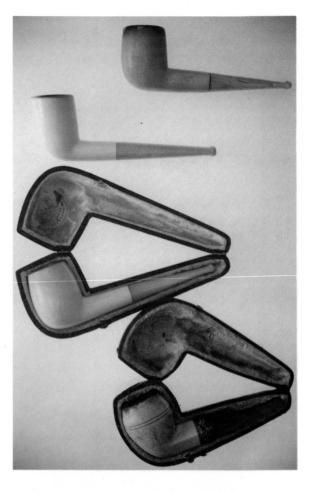

Top-Meerschaum Pipe, 5" x 2", First Middle-
Meerschaum Pipe, 5½" x 2" by K-B&B, Second
Middle-Meerschaum Pipe with Case, 5¼" x 2",
Bottom-Meerschaum Pipe with Case, 4¾" x 2"

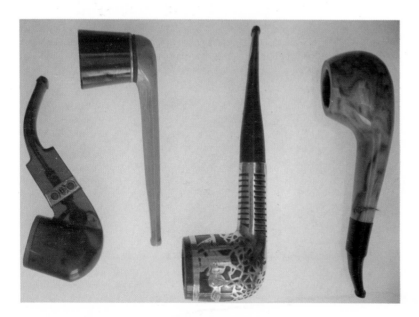

Left-Bakelite Pipe, 4¼" x 1½",
Left Middle-Bakelite Pipe-5" x 1¾", Right
Middle-Wooden Pipe with Silver Overlay,
6" x 1⅞", Right-Catalinor Bakelite Pipe, #245
Made in Belgium, Hilson Fantasia

190

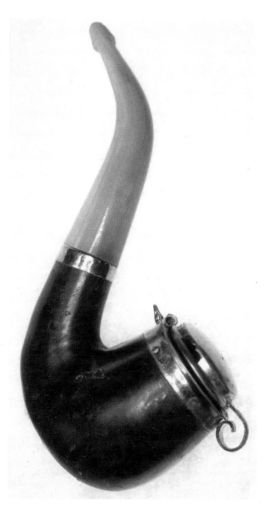

Ivory Mouth Piece with Lid, 4¹/₂" x 1" x 3"

Top-Wooden Pipe with Lid, 4¹/₂" x 3¹/₂", Bottom-
Wood Carved Pipe with Lid of Mans Face, 4" x 6¹/₂"

Brass Oriental Opium Pipe,
7³/₄" x 1¹/₄" x 2¹/₄"

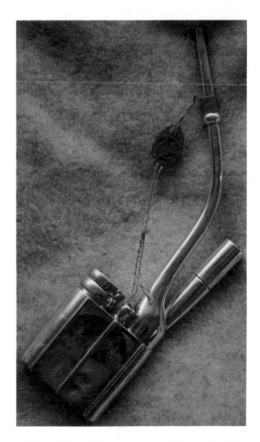

Silver Plated Opium Pipe, China, 10¹/₂"

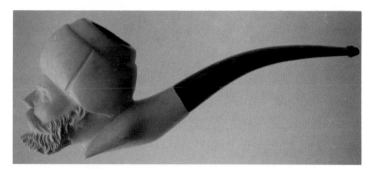

Meerschaum, 6⁵⁄₈"

Ivory Pipe with Woodcase, Pipe-5³⁄₄" x 3",
Case 8" x 3¹⁄₂" x 2¹⁄₂"

Top-Meerschaum, 6³⁄₄" x 3¹⁄₈",
Bottom-O-Boy by K-B&B, 2¹⁄₂" x ⁷⁄₈",
Top Shown for Size Comparison

Jumbo Wood Carved Oriental Dragon Pipe Small Pipe is to
Show Size Comparison, 5" x 10³⁄₄" x 3¹⁄₂"

Bakelite Smoking Set with Case, Pipe-5¹⁄₄" x 1¹⁄₂",
Cigarette Holder-2³⁄₄", Cigar Holder 2¹⁄₂"

Top-Meerschaum Pipe with 14k Gold Trim,
5¹⁄₂" x 2¹⁄₂", Bottom-Bakelite Pipe with
Gold Trim, 4" x 3"

Reproduction Pipes

These new pipes are being made by the thousands. Most are sold in modern upbeat tobacco shops.
___**BEWARE**___ many are being aged and sold as old pipes, so be very careful when buying.

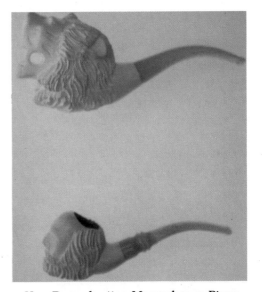

New Reproduction Meerschaum Pipes

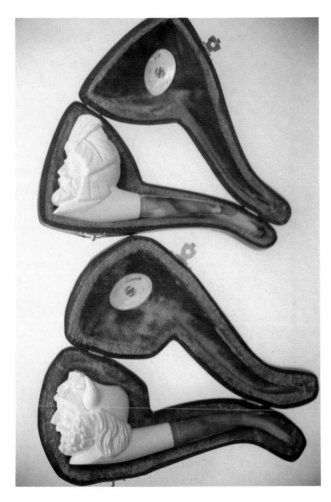

New Production Meerschaum Pipes

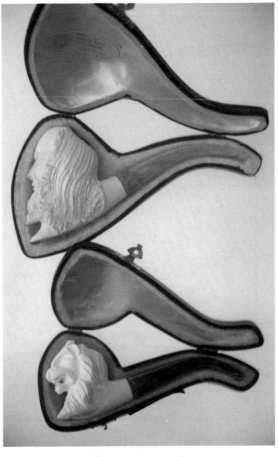

New Reproduction Meerschaum Pipes

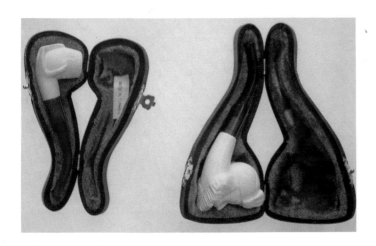

New Reproduction Meerschaum Pipes

Pipe Rests

Humidor and Pipe with Assortment of Pipes,
8½" x 5" x 6¼"

Akro Agate Pipe Holder, 8" x 5" x 3¼"

Golfer Pipe Rest, and Akro Agate with
Pipe Holder, Rest-4" x 3", Holder-4" x 6½"

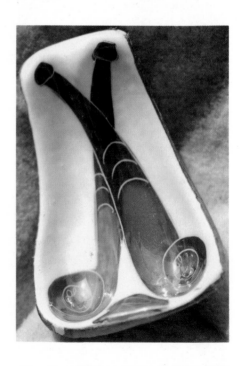

Pipe Rest Pottery Made in Italy, 3¼"

Bronze Ashtray with Two Pipe Rests, 8$^{1/2}$" x 4" x 5"

Bronze Ashtray with Two Pipe Rests, 8$^{1/2}$" x 4" x 5"

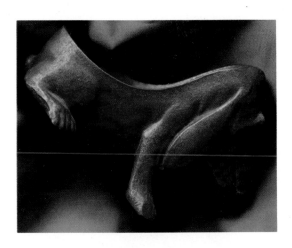

Dog Pipe Holder Brass, 3" x 4$^{1/4}$" x 2$^{1/4}$"

Pipe Rests Composition, Top-1" x 4$^{3/4}$" x 3$^{5/8}$",
Bottom-1$^{3/4}$" x 5$^{1/4}$" x 2$^{1/4}$"

Calabash Pipe and Rest, 6$^{1/4}$" x 2$^{5/8}$" x 6"

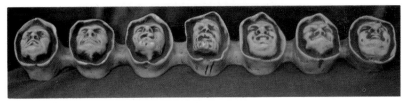

Unusual Monk Faces Wall Pipe Holder, 3$^{1/4}$" x 2$^{1/2}$" x 19$^{3/4}$"

Cardboard Display, 8³/₄" x 8¹/₄"

3³/₄"

Tobacco Humidor Glass Bottom, Lid Bronze, By
HANDEL, 5¹/₄" x 5"

Price Guide

Page 9
All on Page-50+
Page 10
All on Page-40-50
Page 11
All on Page-40-50
Except Figures 125+
Page 12
No. 539401-60+
No. 539402-40+
No. 539403-40+
No. 539404-60+
No. 539405-40+
No. 539406-60+
Page 13
No. 539301-60+
No. 539302-60+
No. 539303-60+
No. 539304-65+
No. 539305-10+
No. 539306-15+
No. 539307-40+
No. 539308-60+
No. 539309-60+
No. 539310-60+
No. 539311-15+
Page 14
No. S1369-100+
No. S1370-40+
No. S1379-90+
No. S134-75+
No. S1381-75+
No. S1383-75+
No. S1380-125+
No. S1371-50+
No. S9390-40+
No. S1393-50+
Page 16
Figures 100+
Others 20-30
Page 18
All on Page-75+
Page 19
Top Left-475
Top Middle-725
Top Right-825
Middle Left-1,800
Middle -1,100
Middle Right-475
Bottom Left-425
Bottom Middle-95
Bottom Right-350
Page 20
No. 2450-10+
No. 2690-40+
No. 2453-40+

No. 1900-30+
No. 1901-40+
No. 2455-20+
No. 2691-50+
No. 2591-30+
No. 3450-35+
No. 3451-40+
No. 2592-40+
Page 21
No. BL4080-30+
No. BL4081-35+
No. BL4082-25+
No. BL4083-25+
No. BL4084-35+
No. BL4085-30+
No. BL4086-40+
No. BL4087-70+
No. BL4088-40+
Page 22
No. BL3962-20+
No. BL3964-35+
No. BL3965-30+
No. BL3966-20+
No. BL3967-25+
No. BS5715-25+
No. BL3969-40+
No. BS5717-45+
Page 23
No. BL4066-75+
No. BL4067-35+
No. BL 4068-30+
No. BL4069-50+
No. BL4070-40+
No. BL4072-50+
No. BL4074-40+
No. BL4075-40+
No. BL4076-60+
No. BL4077-25+
No. BL4078-100+
Page 24
No. 6581-30+
No. 6577-20+
No. 6576-15+
No. 6579-40+
No. 6580-10+
No. 12-10+
No. 6582-30+
No. 6583-50+
No. 6578-40+
No. 6585-75+
Page 25
Top Left-25
Top Middle-75
Top Right-75
Middle Left-50
Middle Right-50
Bottom Left-50

Bottom Right-75
Page 26
Top Left-25
Top Middle-10
Top Right-50
Middle Left-25
Middle Right-25
Bottom Left-35
Bottom Middle-25
Bottom Right-25
Page 27
Top-75
Bottom Left-75
Bottom Right-75
Page 28
Top Left-35
Middle Left-55
Top Right-85
Middle Right 550
Bottom-75 (Each)
Page 29
No. 202-15+
No. 203-15+
No. 204-15+
No. 501-10+
No. 502-10+
No. 405-45+
No. 403-45+
No. 402-45+
Page 30
Top Left-65+
Top Right-65+
Middle Left-75+
Middle Right-75+
Bottom Left-35+
Bottom Right-20+
Page 31
No. T21301-20+
No. T21302-20+
No. T21303-20+
No. T21304-40+
Page 32
All on Page-40+
Page 33
All in Mint or Unused
Condition -750+
Page 34
All in Mint or Unused
Condition-750+
Page 35
No. 8156-75+
No. 8157-75+
No. 8158-60+
No. 8159-60+
No. 8160-40+

No. 8161-40+
No. 8162-60+
No. 8163-75+
No. 8164-45+
No. 8165-50+
No. 8166-40+
No. 8167-40+
Page 36
Top Left-25+
Middle Left-30+
Bottom Left-35+
Top Right-50+
Bottom Right-65+
Page 37
No. 6-20+
No. 9-20+
No. 90-25+
No. 5-30+
No. 65-25+
No. 650-25+
No. 7-40+
Page 38
No. 5860-75+
No. 5859-75+
No. 5862-75+
No. 5863-40+
No. 5870-45+
No. 5864-35+
No. 5868-60+
No. 5861-70+
No. 5869-40+
No. 5866-40+
No. 5867-40+
No. 5865-40+
Page 39
No. 7336-100+
No. 7339-60+
No. 7338-60+
No. 7340-60+
No. 7341-60+
No. 7342-60+
No. 7344-75+
No. 7345-75+
No. 7346-75+
Page 40
All in Top Row-50+
All in Middle Row-50+
No. 563009-40+
No. 563010-75+
No. 563011-40+
No. 536012-40+
Page 41
All in Top Row-50+
No. 817210-50+
No. 563204-150+
No. 563204$^{1/2}$-50+

No. 563205-175+
No. 563205$^{1/2}$-65+
No. 563206-30+
No. 563206$^{1/2}$-100+
No. 860304-50+
No. 860305-50+
No. 860307-35+
No. 860303-100+
No. 860308-25+

Page 42
No. 860201-60+
No. 860202-60+
No. 860203-60+
No. 860204-50+
No. 860205-75+
No. 860206-100+
No. 860207-40+
No. 860208-40+
No. 860209-50+
No. 860210-100+
No. 860211-40+
No. 860212-25+
No. 860213-30+
No. 860214-30+
No. 860215-30+

Page 43
No. 562801-35+
No. 562802-20+
No. 562803-40+
No. 562804-15+
No. 566006-35+
No. 566007-25+
No. 561605-40+
No. 566009-75+
No. 566011-40+
No. 566012-40+
No. C.C.5782-30+
No. S8809-10+
No. S8807-20+
No. J8825-15+
No. S8808-10+

Page 44
No. MH48-275+
No. MH61-125+
No. MH75-100+
No. MH47-600+
No. MH9-200+
No. MH51-650+
No. MH1-135+
No. MH2-175+

Page 45
No. T207-30+
No. 6584-75+
No. 6546-40+
No. 6542-45+
No. 8850-40+
No. 8851-40+
No. 8856-60+
No. 6543-30+
No. 6549-40+

Page 46
All on Page-4+

Page 47
Top-7+
Bottom-2+

Page 48
Top-5+
Bottom-5+

Page 49
Top-7+
Bottom-7+

Page 50
Top Left-4+
Top Right-5+
Bottom-4+

Page 51
Top Left-5+
Top Right-3+
Bottom Left-5+
Bottom Right-10+

Page 52
Top-5+
Bottom-5+

Page 53
Top-5+
Bottom-5+

Page 54
Top-7+
Bottom-7+

Page 55
Top Left-10+
Top Right-10+
Bottom-6+

Page 56
Top-5+
Bottom-5+

Page 57
Top Left-250+
Top Right-750+
Bottom-10+

Page 58
Top-40+
Bottom Left-70+
Bottom Right-90+

Page 59
Top Left-20+
Bottom Left-10+
Top Right-10+
Middle Right-150+
Bottom Right-30+

Page 60
Top Left-200-300
1 Middle Left-35-40
2 Middle Left-1,000-1,500
Bottom-200-300
Top Right-1,000-1,500
Bottom Right-400-500

Page 61
Middle Left-5+
Bottom Left-15+
Top Right-15+
Bottom Right-25+

Page 62
Flier-15-20+
Machine Itself-1,000+

Page 63
Top Left-125-165
Top Middle-1,000

Top Right-40+
Bottom-150+

Page 64
Top Left-25+
Middle Left-25+
Bottom Left-35+
Top Right Picture-
  top-50+
  middle-25+
  bottom-25+
Bottom Right-12+

Page 65
(Prices for Unused Punch Boards)
Top Left-75+
Top Right-40+
Bottom Left-50+
Bottom Middle-10+
Bottom Right-30+

Page 66
(Prices for Unused Punch Boards)
Top Left-35+
Top Right-35+
Bottom Left-35+
Bottom Right-25+

Page 67
(Prices for Unused Punch Boards)
Top Left-40+
Top Right-30+
Bottom Left-15+
Bottom Right-50+

Page 68
Top Left-10+
Top Right Picture-
  top-2+
  bottom-5+
Bottom-2+(Each)

Page 69
Top Left Picture-
  top left -3+
  top right -3+
  bottom left -3+
  bottom right-2+
Top Right-3+(Each)
Bottom-10+

Page 70
All on Page-6+ (Each)

Page 71
Top Left-30+
Top Right-30+
Bottom Left-5+
Bottom Right-5+

Page 72
All on Page-3 (Each)

Page 73
All on Page-3 (Each)

Page 74
All on Page 10+

Page 75
Top Left-10+
Top Right-15+
Bottom Left-15+
Bottom Right-15+

Page 76
Top Left-10+
Top Right-25+
Bottom Left-10+
Bottom Right-10+

Page 77
All on Page-10+(Each)

Page 78
All on Page-2+ (Each)

Page 79
Top Left-5+ (Each)
Top Right-2+ (Each)
Bottom Left-15+
Bottom Right-15+

Page 80
Top Left-5+ (Each)
Top Right-20+
Bottom Left-20+
Bottom Right-10+

Page 81
Top Left-50+
Top Right-20+
Bottom Left-30+
Bottom Right-10+

Page 82
Top Left-75+
Top Right-50+
Bottom Left-40+
Bottom Right-50+

Page 83
Top-75+
Bottom-25+

Page 84
Top Left Picture-
  all 5+ except
  top left-10+
  middle left-10+
Bottom Left Picture-
  left-35+
  right-45+
Top Middle-50+
Middle Picture-
  left-40+
  right-35+
Bottom Middle-40+
Top Right-10+ (Each)
Bottom Right Picture-
  top left-10+
  top right-15+
  middle left-40+
  middle right-5+
  bottom-5+

Page 85
Top Left Picture-
  top-6+
  bottom-7+
Top Right Picture-
  top left-15+
  top right-5+
  middle left-5+
  middle right-50+
  bottom left-15+
  bottom right-40+
Middle-25+

Bottom Left-25+(Set)
Bottom Right-65+

Page 86
Top Left-40+
Top Middle-15+
Top Right-50+
Bottom Left Picture
  top left-15+
  top right-10+
  bottom-5+
Bottom Right-70+

Page 87
Top Left-75+
Top Middle-65+
Top Right-65+
Middle Left-25+
Middle-20+
Middle Right-7+
Bottom Left-25+
Bottom Right-25+

Page 88
Top Left-90
Top Right-75-100
Middle Left-100
Middle-50
Middle Right-8+
Bottom Left-100
Bottom Right-150+

Page 89
Top-400-500

Page 90
Top Left-7+
Top Middle-50+
Top Right-15+
Middle Left-25+
Middle-20+
Middle Right-15+
Bottom Left-35+
Bottom Right-60+

Page 91
Top Left-35+
Top Right-35+
Middle Left-75+
Middle Right-40+
Bottom Left-60+
Bottom Right-30+

Page 92
Top Left-35+
Top Right-20+
Middle Left-100+
Middle Right-35+
Bottom Left-10+
Bottom Right-15+

Page 93
Top Left-20+
Top Right-40+
Middle Left-30+
Middle Right-150+
Bottom Left-40+
Bottom Right-10+

Page 94
Top Left-25+
Top Right-20+
Bottom Left-20+

Bottom Middle-100+
Bottom Right-75+

Page 95
Top-40+
Middle-40+
Bottom-75+

Page 96
Top Left-35+
Top Right-15+
Bottom Left-100+
Bottom Right-20+

Page 97
Top Left-1-5+ (Each)
Top Right-15+
Bottom Left-50+
Bottom Right-15+

Page 98
Left-12+
Right-30+

Page 99
Top-25+
Bottom Left-35+
Bottom Right-100+

Page 100
Top Left-75+
Bottom Left-20+
Top Right-60+
Middle-75+
Bottom Right-40+

Page 101
Top Left-65+
Top Right-75+
Bottom Left-75+
Bottom Right-25+

Page 102
Top Left-400+
Top Right-50+
Bottom Left-20+
Bottom Right-75+

Page 103
Top-150+
Bottom-60+

Page 104
Top Left-40+
Top Right-50+
Bottom-40+

Page 105
Top-250+
Bottom-50+

Page 106
Top Left Picture-
  top-15+
  bottom-20+
Top Right-45+
Bottom-50+

Page 107
Top Left Picture-
  top left-25+
  top right-45+
  middle left-5+
  middle right-7+
  bottom-6+
Top Right Picture-

  top left-10+
  top right-5+
  bottom-5+
Bottom Left Picture-
  top left-5+
  top right-10+
  bottom left-10+
  bottom right-10+
Bottom Middle-55+
Bottom Right Picture-
  top left-5+
  top right-20+
  bottom left-4+
  bottom right-5+

Page 108
Top Left-6+ (Each)
Middle Left-40+
Bottom Left-15+
Top Right Picture-
  top left-10+
  top right-10+
  bottom left-25+
  bottom right-15+
Bottom Right Picture-
  top left-10+
  top right-6+
  bottom left-6+
  bottom right-8+

Page 109
Top Left-25+
Bottom Left-15+(Each)
Right Picture-
  top-50+
  bottom-75+

Page 110
Top Left Picture-
  top left-75-100
  bottom right-75-125
Top Right-130-150
Bottom Right Picture-
  top-90+
  bottom-125+

Page 111
Top Picture-
  top-35+
  bottom-40+
Bottom-80+

Page 112
Top Picture-
  top-25+
  bottom-40+
Bottom-20+ (Each)

Page 113
All on Page-200+(Each)

Page 114
All on Page-150+(Each)

Page 115
All on Page-200+(Each)

Page 116
Top Left-15+
Top Right-15+
Bottom Left-10-25+ (Each)
Bottom Right-2-5 (Each)

Page 117
Top Picture-
  top left-30+
  top right-20+
  middle-10+
  bottom left-30+
  bottom right-30+
  left-40+
Bottom Picture-
  top left-15+
  bottom left-50+
  top-20+
  top middle-20+
  bottom middle-20+
  bottom-25+

Page 118
Top Left-15+
Middle Left-Reference
Only
Bottom Left Picture-
  no. 1-30+
  no. 2-50+
  no. 3-20+
  no. 4-20+
  no. 5-15+
Top Right Picture-
  numbers 1-7 and
  10 are 5-10+
  no. 8-20+
  no. 9-25+
Bottom Right Picture-
  no. 1-30+
  no. 2-15+
  no. 3-15+
  no. 4-25+
  no. 5-30+
  no. 6-75+

Page 119
Top Left-20+
Top Right-45+
Bottom-50+

Page 120
Top Left-50+
Middle Left-20+
Bottom Left-10+
Top Right-20+
Bottom Right-15+

Page 121
Top Left-25+
Top Right-35+
Bottom-75+

Page 122
Top Left-250-350
Top Right-250-350
Bottom Left-850-1,000
Bottom Right-350-500

Page 123
Top-75+
Middle Left-50+
Middle Right-30+
Bottom Left-25+
Bottom Right-35+

Page 124

Top Left-40+
Middle Left-40+
Bottom Left-10+
Middle (toilet seat)-10+
Top Right-20+
1 Middle Right-25+
2 Middle Right-15+
Bottom Right-25+
Page 125
Top Left-50+
Top Right-75+
Bottom-25+
Page 126
All-25+ except
Top Left-20+
2 Middle Right-20+
Page 127
Top Left-15+
Top Right-10+
Bottom Left-5+
Bottom Right-20+
Page 128
Top Picture
   left-40+
   middle-10+
   right-10+
Middle Left-10+(Each)
Middle Right-45+
Bottom Left-50+
Bottom Middle-8+
Bottom Right-25+
Page 129
Top Left-10+
Top Right-5+ (Each)
Middle Left-6+
Middle Right-4+
Bottom Left-15+
Bottom Right-10+
Page 130
Top-5+ (Each)
1 Middle Left-6+(Each)
2 Middle Left-10+
Bottom Left Picture-
   left-20+
   right-8+
1 Middle Right-10+(Pair)
2 Middle Right-20+ (Set)
Bottom Right Picture-
   left-5+
   right-20+
Page 131
Left-200+
Right-100+
Page 132
Top Left-15+
Top Right-40+
Bottom Left-20+
Bottom Right-15+
Page 133
Top Left-15+
Top Right-15+
Bottom Left-15+
Bottom Right-20+

Page 134
Top-250+
Bottom-400+
Page 135
Top Left-60+
Top Right-40+
Bottom Left-75+
Bottom Right-75+
Page 136
   (Prices are for Sets)
Top Left-15+
Top Right-15+
Bottom Left-25+
Bottom Middle-20+
Bottom Right-10+
Page 137
   (Prices are for Sets)
Top Left-25+
Top Right-25+
Bottom Left-75+
Bottom Right-30+
Page 138
   (Prices are for Sets)
Top Left-40+
Top Middle-15+
Top Right-20+
Left Middle-10+
Bottom Left-45+
Bottom Right-35+
Page 139
   (Prices are for Sets)
Top Left-75+
Top Right-35+
Bottom Left-35+
Bottom Right-40+
Page 140
   (Prices are for Sets)
Top Left-20+
Top Middle-65+
Top Right-40+
Bottom Left-30+
Bottom Right-40+
Page 141
   (Prices are for Sets)
Top Left-20+
Top Right-25+
Bottom Left-10+
Bottom Right-15+
Page 142
   (Prices are for Sets)
Top Left-30+
Top Right-50+
Bottom Left-25+
Bottom Right-40+
Page 143
   (Prices are for Sets)
Top Left-75+
Top Right-125+
Bottom Left-75-100
Bottom Right-125-150
Page 144
   (Prices are for Sets)
Top Left-75+
Top Right-35+

Bottom Left-50+
Middle Right-100+
Bottom Right-25+
Page 145
Top Left-250+
Top Right-40+
Bottom Left-30+
Bottom Right-40+
Page 146
Top Left-75+
Top Right-100+
Bottom-125+
Page 147
Top Left-10+
Middle Left-10+
Bottom Left-25+
Top Right-20+
Bottom Right-10+
Page 148
Top Left Picture-
   top-40+
   bottom-55+
Top Right-15+
Bottom Right-5+
Bottom-40+
Page 149
Top Picture-
   top-3+
   bottom-15+
Middle Left-4+
Bottom Left-3+
Middle (Marlboro)-10+
Bottom Right-10+(Each)
Page 150
Top-6+
Middle Left-30+
Middle Right-20+
Bottom Left-5+
Bottom Right-8+
Page 151
Top-22+
Bottom Left-30+
Bottom Right-20+
Page 152
Top Left-25+
Top Right-35+
Middle Left-7+
Middle Right-15+
Bottom Left-50+
Bottom Right-15+
Page 153
Top Left-35+
Top Right-15+
Middle Left-20+
Bottom Left-45+
Bottom Right-40+
Page 154
Top Left-30+
Top Right-20+
Bottom Left-20+
Bottom Right-10+
Page 155
Top Left-20+
Top Right-15+

Bottom Left-25+
Middle Right-25+
Bottom Right-10+
Page 156
Top Left-20+
Top Right-50+
Bottom Left-20+ (Each)
Bottom Right-50+
Page 157
Top Left-20+
Top Right-4+
Bottom Left-35+
Middle Right-15+
Bottom Right-20+
Page 158
   ROW 1
Left-15+
Middle-10+
Right-35+
   ROW 2
Left-35+
Right-20+
   ROW 3
Left-20+
Top Middle-15+
Bottom Middle-15+
Right-15+
Page 159
Top Left-8+
Top Right-8+
Middle Left-12+
Middle Right-10+
Bottom-10+
Page 160
Top Left-12+ (Set)
Top Right-10+ (Each)
Bottom Left-15+
Bottom Right-8+
Page 161
Top Left-75+
Top Right-75+
Bottom Left-30+
Bottom Right-40+
Page 162
Top Left-25+
Top Right-20+
Bottom Left-25+
Bottom Right-10+
Page 163
Top Left-20+
Middle-40+
Bottom-40+
Page 164
Top Left-100+
Top Right-50+
Bottom-30+
Page 165
Top Left-75+
Top Right-65+
Bottom Left-75+
Middle Right-40+
Bottom Right-85+
Page 166
Top Left-30+

Top Right-15+
Bottom Left-20+
Bottom Right-15+
Page 167
Top Left-28+
Top Right-20+
Middle Left-20+
Middle Right-10+
Bottom-10+
Page 168
Top Left-10+
Top Right-40+
Middle Left-25+
Middle Right-10+
Bottom Left-30+
Bottom Right-35+
Page 169
Top Left-10+
Top Right-20+
Middle Left-35+
Middle Right-10+
Bottom Left-45+
Bottom Middle-30+
Bottom Right-30+
Page 170
Top Left-65+
Top Right-125+
Bottom Left-10+
Bottom Right-65+
Page 171
Top-90+
Bottom Left-28+
Bottom Right-75+
Page 172
Top Left-75+
Top Right-50+
Bottom-250+
Page 173
Top-75+
Bottom-50+
Page 174
Top Left Picture-
    all-15+ except
    bottom left-28+
Middle Left Picture-
    left-65+
    right-85+
Bottom Left-20+
Top Right Picture-
    top-15+
    middle-75+
    bottom-16+
Middle Right-15+
Bottom Middle-35+
Bottom Right-35+
Page 175
Top Left Picture-
    all-15+ except
    top-30+
    pocono-28+
Bottom Left-30+
Top Right Picture-
    top-30+
    middle-24+

bottom-24+
Middle Right-20+
Bottom Right-100+
Page 176
Top Left Picture-
    top left-15+
    top middle-5+
    top right-10+
    middle left-15+
    middle-25+
    middle right-10+
    bottom left-5+
    bottom middle-10+
    bottom right-20+
Top Right-All 15-20+
Bottom Left Picture-
    top left-7+
    top middle-50+
    top right-25+
    middle left-35+
    middle-18+
    middle right-8+
    bottom left-8+
    bottom middle-20+
    bottom right-15+
Bottom Right Picture-
    top row-8+ (Each)
    middle left-8+
    middle-15+
    middle right-5+
    bottom left-10+
    bottom middle-10+
    bottom right-8+
Page 177
Top Left Picture-
    top left-10+
    top middle-18+
    top right-20+
    middle left-15+
    middle -12+
    middle right-15+
    bottom left-10+
    bottom middle-20+
    bottom right-8+
Top Right Picture-
    top left-10+
    top middle-10+
    top right-30+
    middle left-8+
    middle-10+
    middle right-20+
    bottom left-12+
    bottom middle-15+
    bottom right-10+
Bottom Picture-
    top left-30+
    top middle-25+
    top right-25+
    middle left-10+
    middle-10+
    middle right-8+
    bottom left-8+
    bottom middle-10+
    bottom right-35+

Page 178
Top Left Picture-
    top left-20+
    top middle-15+
    top right-65+
    middle left-11+
    middle -15+
    middle right-15+
    bottom left-10+
    bottom middle-15+
    bottom right-10+
Bottom Left Picture-
    top left-30+
    top middle-25+
    top right-25+
    middle left-5+
    middle-15+
    middle right-8+
    bottom left-28+
    bottom middle-8+
    bottom right-20+
Bottom Right Picture-
    top left-10+
    top middle-40+
    top right-10+
    middle left-5+
    middle-20+
    middle right-8+
    bottom left-8+
    bottom middle-15+
    bottom right-20+
Page 179
Top Left Picture-
    top left-14+
    top middle-20+
    top right-8+
    middle left-8+
    middle -15+
    middle right-5+
    bottom left-30+
    bottom middle-20+
    bottom right-20+
Bottom Left Picture-
    top left-10+
    top middle-8+
    top right-5+
    middle left-10+
    middle-15+
    middle right-10+
    bottom left-17+
    1 bottom middle-9+
    2 bottom middle-20+
    bottom right-20+
Page 180
Top Left Picture-
    top left-40+
    top middle-9+
    top right-9+
    middle left-30+
    middle-30+
    middle right-8+
    bottom left-15+
    bottom middle-8+
    bottom right-8+
Top Right-8-10+ (Each)

Bottom Left Picture-
    all-8+ except-
    top left-15+
    bottom middle-25+
Bottom Right Picture-
    all-8+ except-
    top left-30+
    middle right-15+
    bottom left-15+
Page 181
Top Left Picture-
    top left-8+
    top middle-8+
    top right-13+
    middle left-8+
    middle-10+
    middle right-15+
    bottom left-20+
    bottom middle-15+
    bottom right-8+
Top Right Picture-
    top left-20+
    top middle-8+
    top right-8+
    middle row-8+ (Each)
    bottom left-7+
    bottom middle-25+
    bottom right-45+
Bottom Left Picture-
    top left-8+
    top middle-14+
    top right-8+
    middle left-8+
    middle-8+
    middle right-35+
    bottom left-20+
    bottom middle-10+
    bottom right-8+
Bottom Right-8-10+ (Each)
Page 182
Top Left Picture-
    top left-30+
    top middle-12+
    top right-21+
    middle left-15+
    middle-8+
    middle right-8+
    bottom left-10+
    bottom middle-8+
    bottom right-8+
Top Right Picture-
    top row-8+ (Each)
    middle left-8+
    middle-20+
    middle right-25+
    bottom left-35+
    bottom middle-30+
    bottom right-10+
Bottom Right-8-10+(Each)
Bottom Left Picture-
    top left-15+
    top middle-10+
    top right-25+
    middle left-10+
    middle-8+

middle right-20+
bottom left-25+
bottom middle-30+
bottom left-12+

Page 183

Top Left Picture-
   top left-11+
   top middle-20+
   top right-50+
   middle left-25+
   middle-25+
   middle right-8+
   bottom row-8+ (Each)
Top Right-8-10+ (Each)
Bottom Left Picture-
   top row-8+ (Each)
   middle left-8+
   middle-10+
   middle right-10+
   bottom left-8+
   bottom middle-19+
   bottom right-20+
Bottom Right Picture-
   top left-8+
   top middle-10+
   top right-10+
   middle left-75+
   middle right-25+
   middle-20+
   bottom left-17+
   bottom middle-12+
   bottom right-10+

Page 184

Top Left Picture-
   top left-8+
   top middle-8+
   top right-18+
   middle left-18+
   middle-8+
   middle right-9+
   bottom left-21+
   bottom middle-15+
   bottom right-8+
Top Right-8-10+ (Each)
Bottom Left Picture
   top row-8+ (Each)
   middle left-8+
   middle-18+
   middle right-10+
   bottom left-9+
   bottom middle-8+
   bottom right-8+
Bottom Right Picture-
   top left-18+
   top middle-8+
   top right-12+
   middle left-12+
   middle-25+
   middle right-30+
   bottom left-10+
   bottom middle-10+
   bottom right-20+

Page 185

Top Left Picture-
   top row-5+ (Each)

middle left-10+
middle-17+
middle right-15+
bottom left-15+
bottom middle-8+
bottom right-8+
Top Right Picture-
   top left-40+
   top middle-20+
   top right-15+
   middle left-20+
   middle-8+
   middle right-8+
   bottom left-8+
   bottom middle-15+
   bottom right-10+
Bottom Left Picture-
   top left-8+
   top middle-35+
   top right-10+
   middle left-10+
   middle-30+
   middle right-20+
   bottom left-15+
   bottom middle-8+
   bottom right-8+
Bottom Right Picture-
   top row-10+ (Each)
   middle left-10+
   middle-10+
   middle-8+
   bottom left-8+
   bottom middle-21+
   bottom right-30+

Page 186

Top Left Picture-
   top left-30+
   top middle-30+
   top right-8+
   middle left-8+
   middle-10+
   middle right-32+
   bottom left-10+
   bottom middle-8+
   bottom right-8+
Top Right Picture
   top left-12+
   top middle-30+
   top right-15+
   middle left-25+
   middle-20+
   middle right-8+
   bottom left-24+
   bottom middle-8+
   bottom right-20+
Bottom Left-15+ (Each)
Bottom Right Picture-
   all-15+ except
   middle left-25+

Page 187

Top Left-55+
2 Middle Left-35+
Bottom Left-30+
Middle (Old Gold)-8+
Middle Right Picture-

top-20+
bottom-10+
Bottom Right-10+

Page 188

Top Left Picture-
   top-30+
   bottom-10+
Bottom Left Picture-
   top-30+
   bottom-35+
Top Right-25+
Bottom Right Picture-
   top-30+
   bottom-35+

Page 189

Top Left Picture-
   all-10+ except
   middle right-20+
   bottom right-30+
Top Right Picture-
   all-10 except
   middle right-20+
Bottom-20+ (Each)

Page 190

Top Left Picture-
   top-40+
   middle-50+
   bottom-65+
Top Right Picture-
   top-35+
   1 middle-25+
   2 middle-50+
   bottom 50+
Bottom Picture-
   left-40+
   1 middle-50+
   2 middle-35+
   right-40+

Page 191

Top Left-35+
Top Right Picture-
   top-15+
   bottom-20+
Bottom Left-75+
Bottom Right-75+

Page 192

Top Left-100+
Top Right-125+
Middle Left Picture-
   top-125+
   bottom-15+
Middle Right-50+
Bottom Left-125+
Bottom Right Picture-
   top-45+
   bottom-100+

Page 193

Reference Only

Page 194

Top Left Picture-
   humidor-25+
   pipes-5+ (each)
Top Right-20+
Bottom Left Picture-

top-10+
bottom-15+
Bottom Right-7+

Page 195

Top Left-15+
Top Right-25+
Middle Left-10+
Middle Right-8+
Bottom Left-15+
Bottom Right-75+

Page 196

Top-10+
Bottom Left-500+
Bottom Right-5+

Price Guide on Lighters

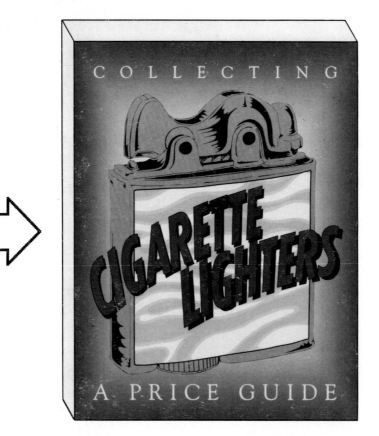

Light up your library with this new book. This volume has over 60 original catalog pages. Included are many original ads, black and white older photos and over 85 pages of living color (over 185 total pages). This book will cover pocket, table, trench, electric, battery and store lighters. All lighters are illustrated or photographed and are priced. If you want to be among the first to have this book GET YOUR ORDERS READY NOW!

$24.95

+ $2.00 shipping for the first book 40¢ for each additional book.
Send Check or Money Order to:
L-W Book Sales, P.O. Box 69, Gas City, IN 46933
Or call 1-800-777-6450 for Visa, Mastercard and C.O.D.
Orders Only!